Brazilian Food

Brazilian Food
Race, Class and Identity in Regional Cuisines

Jane Fajans

London • New York

English edition
First published in 2012 by
Berg
Editorial offices:
50 Bedford Square, London WC1B 3DP, UK
175 Fifth Avenue, New York, NY 10010, USA

Berg is an imprint of Bloomsbury Publishing Plc.

Library of Congress Cataloging-in-Publication Data
A catalogue record for this book is available from the Library of Congress.

British Library Cataloguing-in-Publication Data
A catalogue record for this book is available from the British Library.

ISBN 978 0 85785 041 6 (Cloth)
       978 0 85785 042 3 (Paper)
e-ISBN 978 0 85785 043 0 (epub)

Typeset by Apex CoVantage, LLC, Madison, WI, USA.
Printed in the UK by the MPG Books Group

www.bergpublishers.com

To Allison, Terry, and
Vanessa

Contents

List of Illustrations

Acknowledgments

As with any work that has extended over many years and many places, I am deeply indebted to countless people. I have made many trips to Brazil in the last half dozen years and my husband, Terry, has accompanied me on virtually all of them. He has been a wonderful partner, terrific explorer, great taster, and indefatigable eater. We have visited new places together and returned to old ones. On several of our trips our daughters, Vanessa and Allison, have joined us. We have enjoyed sharing this part of our lives and careers with them, and they have come to love the country and the project as much as we have. All three of these wonderful family members have assisted me in the conceptualization and production of this book. I especially want to thank Alli and Terry for their readings and suggestions through multiple drafts of these chapters.

My Brazilian family of Maria José and Tinôco warmly accepted me into their extended family when I was studying Portuguese in Salvador. The meals we ate together are some of the warmest memories I have and, of course, some of the best culinary examples I have experienced. Another long-lasting and wonderful friend in Salvador is Mariaugusta Rosa Rocha, who first taught me to make *moqueca* and then taught me how to celebrate the *Festa de Yemanja* in grand style.

In Rio de Janeiro many friends got on board to help me learn about food, culture, and family. I want to thank Aparecida Vilaça, José Padilha, and Eduardo Viveiros de Castro, all of whom shared meals, stories, and ideas with me. Each of these friends had suggestions about where to go, what to see, and what to eat. I thank them all.

São Paulo is usually our first stop in Brazil and often our last as well. Good friends like Dominique and Richard Gallois are important connections in this city. Clarice Cohn has given us extended hospitality and shown us interesting neighborhoods and restaurants as well as good music. Gabriela Masciola introduced me to the haute cuisine world of São Paulo and the community of exciting chefs and restaurants. I really appreciate her introductions to Alex Atala, Ana Luisa Trajano, and others, and look forward to future adventures with her. My thanks also to Alex Atala for a wonderful tasting meal, fascinating conversation, and his critical study of Levi-Strauss's theories of the cultural basis of cuisine (Atala n.d.).

Longtime friend, former student, and "big sister" to my daughters, Leda Martins, welcomed us into her family in Brasília. Her parents, Maria and Julio Martins, gave us extended hospitality. Maria gave me some very important cooking lessons. On the other side of Brasília we enjoyed extended time with Carmen Figueiredo and

Rodrigo Balbueno, who also hosted us with warmth and advice. Carmen and Rodrigo had previously lived in Porto Alegre, where they introduced us to the strong ethnic cuisines of the Southern regions and the important *churrasco* cultures of the South. Brasília has a large anthropological community with many people who like to eat and drink, talk and work. I'd like to thank Esther Katz; Robert Miller and his wife, Carla; Enzo Lauriola; and Patricia Mendonça de Rodrigues for spending time with us, and helping us think about food, identity, and regional differences.

Our contacts in Curitiba started with Marcel and Natalia Taminato and spread to their parents, Marie and Hiro Taminato. The Taminatos seem to know everyone in that city and helped us meet and talk with a great variety of people across many ethnic communities and many professions and interests. One contact they made for me was with Ivan Koch who generously spent time describing the food and culture of Paraná, about which he has written extensively.

Over many visits to Belém, I have appreciated the experience and knowledge of Louis Forline and his wife, Amália; Paulo Martins; and Ofir Oliveira. I also want to thank Pascale de Robert for pricking my interest in *tacaca*, Carmen Rial for her hospitality and ethnographic counsel in Florianopolis, and Silvia Martins for her advice and guidance in a wonderful visit to Maceio.

Since my husband, Terry, has worked with the Kayapó Indians for fifty years, we have many friends among their villages. I have been privileged to know and learn from Megaron Txukarramãe, Yabuti Mentukitre, Ropni Mentuktire, and Bedjai Txukarramãe.

Finally, in Ithaca, I'd like to thank Luciana Ferreira for her help, Marcus Smolka and Beatriz Almeida for the wonderful Brazilian meals they have provided, and the nostalgia we all feel for Brazil on cold winter afternoons.

I want to thank CU-Advance and the Department of Anthropology Cornell University for grants to support this research.

Boa Vista

Roraima

Amapá
Macapá

Belém

São Luís

Fortaleza

Rio Grande
do Norte

Amazonas

Manaus

Pará

Maranhão

Teresina Ceará

Natal

Paraíba

João Pessoa

Piauí

Pernambuco

Recife

Acre

Rio Branco

Porto Velho

Palmas

Alagoas

Maceió

Rondônia

Mato Grosso

Tocantins

Bahia

Aracaju

Sergipe

Salvador

Goiás

Cuiabá

Brasília

Goiânia

Minas Gerais

Mato Grosso
do Sul

Belo Horizonte

Espírito Santo

States of Brazil

Campo Grande

São Paulo

Vitória

São Paulo

Rio de Janeiro

Paraná

Rio de Janeiro

Curitiba

Santa Catarina

Florianópolis

Rio Grande do Sul

Porto Alegre

−1−

Introduction

Sea and sun, *samba* and soccer, and nowadays, coffee, soy, ethanol, and oil: these are the associations that the name *Brazil* evokes. Visual and sonorous vignettes of a huge and varied nation, they highlight Brazil's increasing presence on the global stage. Brazil is a nation of continental expanse, and enormous variation in geography and climate and rich diversity in its constituent cultures and languages. Inside its boundaries are distinctive regions, each with its own customs, history, and unique identity. In many cases, food, beverages, dishes, and festivals play important parts in defining the character and cohesiveness that underpins a region's distinctiveness. Food also plays a part in defining the region's shared identity with the encompassing nation-state. Among other cultural markers, regions are known for their cuisine, their local ingredients, and the festive occasions that showcase both. While regional foods embody the community, the *terroir*, and the essence of a place, food is also easily transportable and such comestibles are frequently found outside their region of origin. When they are found in new locations, these transports may convey symbolic properties about the region from which they come and the people who traditionally prepare and consume them. Alternatively, culinary transplants may shed such specific characteristics and take on new symbolic and social properties as components of the new cultural identities in which they become included.

In this global age, cuisine is fundamental for understanding notions of identity, regional cohesion, and the presentation of national culture to outsiders. The great Danish chef René Redzepi started exploring the idea of regional identity. He asked "What is a region? What is the sum of the people we are, the culture we are? What does it taste like?" (Kramer 2011). This book explores the role that food plays in the construction of identity on both the regional and national level through key case examples. Through the lens of these studies, I examine these same questions and look at the role that food and food events play as media of social relations, in constructing notions of *terroir*, and as revealing perceptions of race, ethnicity, class, gender, and other features of identity.

Gastro-tourism and culinary exports are features of an increasingly globalized society. Several iconic ingredients and dishes have managed to transcend their regional origins to become integral in national and international perceptions of Brazil. Because my emphasis in this book is on the role of cuisine in the construction of identity, I do not examine the many aspects of food production and exportation that have made Brazil such an important player in the world market (e.g., commodities like soy or beef). To highlight the salient nexus of culture and cuisine, I have selected particular products, some of which have become synonymous with Brazil abroad, such as *açaí*, and tracked the variation and evolution of their uses, values, and perceptions as they move beyond their points of origin.

Each chapter is a study of the way that aspects of regional identity are created and then parlayed into a wider network of meaning and value. The focus is one that should be familiar to many American and Europeans analysts: how does a concept of nationality coexist in a dialectical relationship with notions of regional identity on the one hand and international and global networks on the other? When applied to the topic of comestibles, a further question becomes how does food become an element in both differentiating and uniting a people?

Why Food? Why Brazil?

I first went to Brazil in 1982 with my husband and infant daughter. At the time I was recently returned from fieldwork in Papua New Guinea and was writing my dissertation on the Baining of East New Britain Province, Papua New Guinea. In my analysis of the Baining, food became an increasingly important component of the day-to-day construction of social life and the meaning of sociality. I was therefore thinking about food much of the time and concomitantly exploring and enjoying the, to me, new cuisine of Brazil. The shift from Baining food to Brazilian food took many years during which time I enjoyed teaching a course on the Anthropology of Food and Cuisine and examining food cultures around the world. Only after studying Portuguese to enjoy trips to Brazil with my husband did I become interested in exploring the topic of Brazilian food as a case example of the food and cuisine subjects that I had been teaching for years. I have been visiting Brazil annually for the last six or seven years. This book evolved from this circuitous route. I begin my analysis in Chapter 1 with a discussion of Bahian food, the unique cuisine that first piqued my interest and curiosity about Brazilian regional cuisines.

Brazilian Food

Looking first at some general ideas about food in Brazil, one in particular stands out. Brazilians feel food should be satisfying and substantial. These qualities are frequently expressed in the word *farta*, "filling" or "satisfying." In conversations with me, numerous Brazilians of different regions and classes mentioned this widespread desire for *comida farta* (filling food) and spoke of it as a pervasive value. Rice and beans are the principal vehicles of *comida farta*. Although rice and beans are not the universal basis of a meal in Brazil, most Brazilians feel that a midday or evening meal is incomplete without them. *Comida farta* in many minds thus tends to mean rice and beans.

The different combinations or configurations by which people meet the need for satisfying food in Brazil, and how these paths meet the expectations of different social groups, is part of the story in this book. We shall begin then with the question of why and whether food can be perceived as fulfilling the quality of *farta* or not.

Comida versus *Alimentação*

Brazilian anthropologist Roberto Da Matta attended graduate school in the United States. When he and his family arrived in Cambridge, Massachusetts, in the early 1960s, it took them awhile to set up a proper household and get used to living in a foreign country. During this time, his young daughter complained that in the United States, they had only *comida* and not *alimentação* (Da Matta 1964). Her pronouncement set her father to thinking about the linguistic and classificatory contrast between these two categories. In Brazil, *comida* refers to the category of foods that are primarily assembled rather than cooked and transformed. *Comida* is food as nourishment whereas *alimentação* is a prepared meal. *Comida* includes sandwiches and salads, fruits and beverages, precisely the sorts of foods that a family with a rudimentary kitchen and a busy schedule might resort to in order to keep the energy up and the children from crying. Da Matta's daughter, however, missed the heavier prepared dishes of beans and meat, rice and *farofa*, roasts and stews, fish and barbecue, of her native Rio de Janeiro. For her, the new home was made even more alien than the new country by the lack of familiar and sustaining dishes that she recognized as *alimentação*. She longed for proper *alimentação*, which could transform an alien place into a comfortable and familiar home. The food she received in the United States was nourishment, but it failed to impart that quality of well-being that is captured by the adjective *farta*. She grasped the distinction by recognizing American food as *comida* but not *alimentação* (hot, prepared, and appropriately filling). As a child, she missed the familiar dishes that until that point had been an inseparable aspect of home. Food helps to make a place a home, although sometimes one does not realize its powers of transformation until it fails to do so. Many people experience this longing or nostalgia for dishes from "home." Certain dishes of one's childhood take on the iconic properties of "comfort food."

This book examines the ways that food helps to make a place a home and how it comes to represent home to those who are "away" from home. Where you are from and what you eat is a significant part of who you are and who are the others that are like you. This is not a unique or new observation; many people, most famously Brillat-Savarin ([1825] 2011), have described how food is part of identity and how one defines one's identity and ethnicity in part through culinary habits. Much of people's awareness of this aspect of life and identity, like so many other components of life, only make themselves apparent when they are absent or transformed. Da Matta's daughter framed her memories of home around food, and Da Matta recognized that even these elementary qualities are a subject for anthropological analysis. Food taken out of its mundane context becomes a marked category and one that demands to be consciously considered.

Food and Identity

Since we are all "what we eat" in the broad sense, our identities are intertwined with our food. Food has both metaphorical and metonymical properties, so it is an apt medium for creating identity. Certain foods are thought to impart more concrete substantive properties and others more symbolic associative ones. Metaphorically, color and shape, spiciness, smell, and location can imbue foods with properties of health, wealth, longevity, or sexual potency, among other significant qualities. Hot foods are often associated with passion; long noodles are associated with longevity in many parts of Asia; rice is associated with abundance because it has multiple grains so it is thrown at weddings to symbolize fertility; almonds are also associated with fertility, springtime, and rebirth because they are the first trees to flower in the spring; round foods are often associated with money and thus of wealth, and so forth. Associations with the sea or forest, connection to deities, the sound of the name, or a connection to history can give food metonymical properties as well. These associative properties adhere to an object because of their proximity to another entity that has symbolic value. Foods associated with deities convey qualities of potency borrowed from the power of these gods. Foods associated with the forest can embody properties of nature and health beyond mere nutritive qualities; foods associated with the sea impart the essence of water, life, and life-giving salt. In many cases, food takes on the symbolic properties of its place of origin, the manner of its production, the characteristics of the producer, and the shape, color, smell, and habitual uses of its material context. French wine, Italian olive oil, and Russian caviar convey the value of authenticity because of their associations with particular places and traditions. Cold-pressed oil, barrel-aged wine, and organic grain garner status through the methods employed in their production. Homestead cheese, handmade sausage, and artisanal preserves are valued because of the labor that goes into them and the association with tradition that convey a connection to the past. By eating such products people consume more than just the nutritive and substantive properties of the food but also ingest the symbolic properties that give them additional value. This process of absorbing the symbolic properties of food and internalizing them creates a relation of metonymy. Food is never just nutrition, it is always imbued with the values of production, kinship, and status; even mass-produced foods gain symbolic value through the advertisements and branding that promote them, and buying or consuming them imparts some of this value to the consumer. When people recognize these qualities of their food, they often feel that they gain value and potency by ingesting it. They metonymically incorporate these qualities into themselves and thus take on aspects of locality, substance, form, tradition, potency, history, and other symbolic properties that are associated with the food they eat. Not all foods are felt to have such distinctive properties, and not all the properties of a particular food are imbued with the same content by all consumers, but most people nevertheless are "what they eat" in this sense or become what they want to be by eating it. This aspect of consumption is sometimes associated with a desire to gain status and distinction through what one consumes and how one selects and discriminates among choices. Whether one is choosing white bread over multigrain or multigrain over white, organic over factory-produced meat, or homemade cookies over bakery cookies, the decision is often enveloped in notions of status, identity, and economic constraints (Bourdieu 1984; Barthes 1968; Terrio 1996; Roseberry 1996). Manifesting a discriminating palate gives a person a reputation for knowledge and taste. Eating is frequently a social act, so what you eat and with whom you eat can mark the kind of person you are (or want others to think you are) and augment your status.

The Taste of Place

Food not only takes on the properties of its color, shape, smell, and status, it also acquires particular qualities through its relation to a particular locale. This quality is what the French call *terroir*, and Amy Trubek (2008) translates as "the taste of place." *Terroir* is a complex concept that combines the climate, soil, exposure, sun, wind, and gradient of a particular property with the particular species of a plant or animal, and the techniques and practices of production (the latter including cultural beliefs and practices). All of these characteristics combine to give a product, be it wine, cheese, meat, or coffee a particular taste. That unique amalgamation of factors results in a recognizable taste that reflects the source and care that have gone into the product. The French initially described this essence and have applied it to particular regions and products within their country. Other countries have followed suit, and many of them have protected the products of a particular *terroir* with legal controls that restrict the right to use particular names to products from that region. While many products reflect a taste of place, not all of them have protected status. Nonetheless, many foods and traditionally made products incorporate the idea of *terroir* into their essence and people use this special identity to mark them as different from similar products from other places. Foods like *açaí, cachaça, tucupi, dendê*, and others discussed in this book are imbued with qualities of place even though Brazil has not instituted protected status on any of these ingredients. People ingest these foods and dishes and take on some of the qualities of the place from which they originate. Many people hanker after the food from their home region and see it as part of their identity.

Identity

Identity has many connotations and has been used differently in different social science disciplines. To begin with, *identity* is a term that people use in practice every day. People use identity to describe shared attributes with others, their relations to people, beliefs, activities, and political and social entities (Brubaker and Cooper 2000: 4–5). But identity is also an analytical term. In anthropology, identity has come to mean the sense of belonging to a particular group on the basis of a vague but generally agreed upon set of criteria: usually including religion, ethnicity, sexuality, place of birth or residence, and general social location (class, region, gender, occupation, age, affiliation, etc.). Identity tends to overlap with a number of other forms of classification but does not necessarily share the same boundaries or same implications. Identities are often created, defined, and employed in settings where one or more people are confronted with others who differ in some or many of the criteria held in common throughout the group. Some analysts prefer to describe these processes as *modes of identification* (MacClancy 2004: 64). Identity and alterity are imbricated in the process of production. Although people often adopt an identity as a marker of themselves and their own cohort, identities are also applied and defined by those who are outside the group. In this book, I look at different levels and types of identity: regional, national, gendered, class, and race. These intersect and overlap but not always in the same way. How people self-identify shifts and changes depending on where they are and with whom they are interacting. As the anecdote about Da Matta's daughter at the beginning of this chapter suggests, the identity of being Brazilian comes into focus much more clearly when one is comparing oneself to non-Brazilians. In such situations, being a *Nordestino* (a person from the Northeast of Brazil) or a *Carioca* (a person from Rio de Janeiro) becomes less relevant when one is no longer in Brazil. Within Brazil, however, being a *Nordestino* takes on relevance when one is no longer in the Northeast but loses explicit relevance when one is with other *Nordestinos*. Being a woman or a man may be part of one's everyday consciousness, but being Jewish or Catholic, or of Japanese or German heritage, may not. Identity shifts between emphasizing sameness and difference.

Debates on identity/alterity have been widespread in anthropology, philosophy, cultural studies, and literary criticism (Baumann and Gingrich 2004). To some degree discourses of identity in disciplines like cultural studies have tended to reduce a great many topics to issues of difference. In anthropology, the notion of context becomes very important, and shifting contexts of various sorts, including social, economic, and political forces, can lead to shifting identities and vice versa. In all of these contexts, individuals are always negotiating their own identities vis à vis others and using implicit frames for defining and adjusting relationships. In reality, many relations are fluid and involve cross-cutting types of status and identity. How individuals identify in different situations depends on many factors that can recede or come to the fore in numerous ways. What a food can impart to a person can also fluctuate. The same food can mark one as a *Nordestino* in general, a hillbilly in particular, an indigenous person, or a sophisticate depending on where and with whom it is consumed.

Brazilian notions of identity are understandably complex but are entwined with associations with region of origin or even one's parents' or grandparents' regions of origin, local residence, occupation, class, race, ethnicity, education, religion, and associations with groups on the basis of elective affinity, such as music, dance, *capoeira*, soccer, and countless others. Mediating between different groups are relations of status, employer/employee, teacher/student, performer/audience, producer/consumer, and so forth. These differences take on added salience as connections are formed or broken through family, employment, migration, religion, and other intervening social factors.

Diversity and Equality

Brazil is a country with great geographical diversity from temperate zones to the tropics and from the Atlantic Ocean to the foothills of the Andes. Upon this geographical diversity is juxtaposed an even greater social diversity. The popular myth is that Brazil is composed of three "races"—the indigenous people, the Europeans, and the Africans. In reality, there are many more. Brazil, like the United States and many European countries, has received immigrants from around the world, from Japan, China, Lebanon, Portugal, Spain, Italy, Germany, Ukraine, and many Latin American countries. Despite this diversity, the myth of the three races persists. Constructed on top of this myth is the belief that Brazil is a "racial democracy" (Skidmore 1993: 216–17; Skidmore 2010: 76–77; Burns 1993: 323; Reichmann 1999). This idea carries the connotation that Brazilians are free from racial prejudice and that everyone in the country has equal rights to all resources. Although patently untrue, this view insists that it is not racial prejudice that impedes individual success or opportunity but class, instead, which constrains success and bars entrance to opportunities (Skidmore 2010: 76–77; Eakin 1997: 116–17). The popular view of inequality in Brazilian society, in other words, acknowledges that class is an important determiner of status, opportunity, and well-being while mitigating race as a significant factor.

Within the denial of racial prejudice, however, lurks the realization that race and color matter. As in a number of Latin American countries, miscegenation is considered an important social phenomenon in Brazil and a key to creating a more homogenous society. Within the notion of racial democracy, the process of "whitening" (*embranquecimento*) holds value for both individuals and society as a whole as the intermixing of races creates a whiter/mulatto general public (Skidmore 1993, 2010: 82–84, 104; Caldwell 2007: 30–31, 90). Although an ideal, the process of miscegenation encounters social impediments across all sectors of the society, since many parents discourage their offspring from marrying someone "too dark" while at the same time hoping they will marry up the social scale by marrying a lighter person (Goldstein 2003: 122–25; Scheper-Hughes 1992). So the fear of darkening is the flip side of the goal of whitening. This apprehension derives from the assumption that darker people have fewer opportunities. This recognition of covert racial prejudice emerges in the widespread ploy that many employers use when hiring people, especially for jobs that will provide the public face of their businesses, such as shop assistants or receptionists, jobs that often do not need many prerequisites to qualify, that the applicant be of "good appearance" (*boa aparencia*) (Edmonds 2010: 109; Goldstein 2003). This term is widely interpreted as a euphemism for light-skinned (Goldstein 2003; Edmunds 2010). Despite denials about overt racism these sorts of attitudes form the basis of many social interactions and expectations.

Despite the persistence of different types of identity in Brazil, there is still a strong, and arguably strengthening, overarching sense of encompassment in a single nation. Politics, media, and sports are important venues in which people across the country share common goals, hopes, and identities. However, a "paradigm of inclusion is the tool of the dominant (white) society" (Sjorslev 2004: 84). So, many of the themes and developments that are seen as Brazilian, from Carnival to the Olympics, from soap operas (*Telenovelas*) to ecotourism, are developed and controlled by the already powerful elites. Despite recent moves toward fuller democratization, Brazil still functions as a hierarchical society in which power is no longer vested in the authoritarian military regime but in which a class of people traditionally accustomed to holding power maintain hegemony. This class is predominantly white, wealthy, and educated. These exclusive structures are well illustrated in some of Da Matta's work on civil behavior (1986, 1987; Da Matta and Hess 1995).

Da Matta discusses how rules and laws are applied unequally and how the poor and marginal people are the ones subject to discipline according to such strictures. The elite and wealthy expect special privileges due to their "exceptional" character or status (Da Matta 1987). Such people can sidestep the system by appealing to their position or their connections to others with higher and more important positions. These forms of "dodging" the rules and regulations, which in all honesty were made for "others," are classified under the Portuguese term *jeito*. To fix the problem or manipulate others to your advantage is to get them to give you a pass (*dar um jeito*). Da Matta ties this sense of privilege in with the common expression "*Você sabe com quem você esta falando?*" ("Do you know to whom you are speaking?") This expression is meant to put the other in his or her place and imply the speaker is of higher status and authority. When used, it implicitly threatens the addressee and suggests he or she may suffer if the higher-status person is not treated with care. This expression can be used up and down the social ladder so people who are put down by those above them will turn around and use this technique on those they believe below them when they judge it to be to their advantage.

While Brazil as a nation does not have rigid rules of caste or apartheid, it does have strong values surrounding social divisions, and different races and classes are kept apart in important ways. In cities, the poor most frequently live on the hills, often very steep ones, and the upper classes live on the flats, often near the beach and sea. The wealthy almost never enter the poor areas commonly known as *favelas*. Poorer people cross over into wealthier spaces, however, often as workers and domestic employees but even in this capacity they are viewed with wary suspicion. Such service workers are kept apart by separate entrances to buildings and apartments and separate elevators. Overt hostility threatens those who cross the line (Goldstein 2003: 109–10; Gillam n.d.: 99). Even within a house or apartment, rich or poor, lighter or darker, employer and employee are separated into social and service areas. Domestic workers (*empregadas* literally meaning "employee" but used to designate domestic workers) shop, cook, and do laundry in the service areas of the home, entering the social areas only to clean and serve. Employers traditionally only enter the service areas to instruct the servants.

Feeding and Food Exchange

Anthropologists tend to see processes of exchange and gift giving as creating social relations and mediating between different parties. Exchange is often viewed as a reciprocal relationship with gift givers becoming receivers at a future point in time. This connection holds true to some extent in Brazil but fails significantly in other ways. Although an intimate relation, the bond between workers and employers remains one where service is exchanged for money, therefore, the relation remains one of abstract wage labor. Despite the fact that *empregadas* cook the employers' food and care for their children, their relationship with their employer falls short of a reciprocal exchange. Domestic workers shop, cook, and prepare food but do not share it in a commensal relationship.[1] If *empregadas* do eat the same food as their employers, they usually eat the leftovers in a separate space. Domestic workers may eat with or feed the children of their employers, but this shared commensality evokes the sense that such employees are more like children than adults, a perception that again separates them from their employers. Donna Goldstein describes the awkwardness of eating with her domestic servant in her book *Laughter out of Place*. The social distance the relationship required was collapsed in this act, and the employer/employee relationship shifted to one of friendship, a relation that could not be accommodated in the more formal business relation. Friendship won out in this case (Goldstein 2003: 40–41). This complex relationship of intimacy and distance, while far from unique, underscores the complex race and class relations in Brazilian communities.

Who eats with whom is also a significant aspect of the social criteria for community. In the microcosm of a home, those who eat together and share sustenance also share deeply penetrating connections encapsulated in the symbol of shared substance. Producing, preparing, and consuming a meal is an act that creates and transforms both the ingredients and those who act and consume them. Those who produce the foods do so as labor, but in contemporary society labor is a multifaceted process. Planting, growing, and harvesting food for the table is no longer an essential part of feeding oneself and one's family. Instead the work involved in acquiring the ingredients for a meal involves shopping in markets or stores. As Marx recognized, a living wage must suffice to fulfill not just the material requirement for a worker's survival, but the extended requirement for the worker to reproduce himself or herself and the larger unit to which he or she belongs. Food, clothing, housing, and education for the laborer and his or her family should all be subsumed in this set of endeavors. Even for those engaged in wage labor, the procurement of food is necessary labor. In capitalism, the laborer earns a wage that serves to enable him or her to meet these needs and provide for the extended network of family (Marx 1978: 156–57).

The connections created by nurturing and providing break down when the provider is not investing in the maintenance of her or his own unit of reproduction but that of an employer. The values of exchange and reciprocity, the creation of connection through commensality and shared substance, become severed from the productive processes of cooking, feeding, and imbuing the food with the value of one's own labor. In this environment the notions of exchange or reciprocity become unhinged from social intimacy. The act of giving such items as food takes on a different meaning if the person who makes the food cannot eat it himself or herself. The symbolic properties of food, the notions of shared substances, the sociality of commensality, are all suppressed in this social context, but certain aspects of symbol and meaning persist even in these tortured relations. The desire to make these exchanges part of a social network, however, frequently overwhelms the structural distance between care-giver and cared-for enabling deep emotional ties to develop. Authors such as Giberto Freyre helped promulgate the notion of the racial democracy, based in large measure on the existence of such deep ties that develop between white children and the darker women (*mãe pretas*) who care for them as children (Freyre [1933] 1986; Skidmore 1993: 191). In addition, the ubiquitous meal of rice, beans, and meat, cooked by lower-class women, often descendants of slaves, undergirds the national sense of a people suffused with its colonial and slave past that is refreshed on a daily basis through the food they all eat. If you are what you eat, then to that extent, in the Brazilian context, you are all the same.

Food and Status

The relationship of food and status has long been a subject of analysis and reflection. As Goody argued several decades ago, people and cultures express inequities through a number of criteria (1982). This mode of displaying distinction through the selection, preparation, and display of food remains significant in Brazil today. The principal diet of 90 percent of the world's population for much of human history has been based on a staple starch such as, but not restricted to, rice, wheat, potato, manioc, barley, or taro, often with a small portion of meat or greens as a relish. The wealthy have usually signaled their distinction by eating a more varied diet, often including rare or hard-to-come-by ingredients (Tannahill 1973). Many of our assumptions about what is valued are based on our evaluation of who eats it. Elites or dominant classes may select foods because they are difficult to acquire. Spices, exotic meats, birds' nests, pigeons' tongues, caviar, and so forth are all foods that have met these criteria. Rich foods in our Western parlance are so termed because they were the choice of the rich.

Even in cases where the wealthy do not eat a diet substantially more varied than the rest of society, they often display their status by eating more than others and by selecting the best quality ingredients for their meals. In fact, they have the ability to determine what is considered the best quality (Bourdieu 1984; Goody 1982; Spittler 1999; Terrio 1996; Roseberry 1996). They also have the luxury to change such evaluations at will.

While a large percentage of Brazilians still rely on a carbohydrate-based diet of rice, beans, and manioc, status and wealth are signaled through the accompaniments to these staples. The national dish, *feijoada*, is a basic rice and bean dish, but can be raised to a higher level through the addition of multiple meats and sausages. A *feijoada completa*, as we will see in Chapter 6, becomes a celebratory meal. As social patterns and norms have shifted, so have the criteria for fine dining. Increasing the quantity of protein (meat or fish) is the most frequent way of elevating the status and prestige of a meal. As we will see in later chapters, some restaurants cater to diners' desires to consume large quantities of varied meats while others entice them with small dishes of exotic ingredients in creative combinations. In these and other cases, the pleasure of consumption is compounded by the pleasure of signaling one's belonging to a community recognized as sophisticated and powerful because of that consumption.

Globalization, media, and new values around cooking and eating have altered consumption around the world. Many of these changes are beneficial: new foodstuffs, vegetables, fruits, starches, new styles of preparation, an appreciation for other cuisines, and new gastronomic techniques applied to familiar foods all broaden the array of choice of what we eat. The double-edged sword of these new choices is that many people have been seduced by diets higher in sugar, fat, salt, and calories, which, along with a lifestyle that is more sedentary, has led to increases in "lifestyle" diseases, many of which are consumption-based. Obesity, high blood pressure, and diabetes have resulted from changing patterns of consumption.

Fortunately, currently many fewer Brazilians than in the recent past are suffering from malnutrition caused by insufficient foods, but other health factors have now become a significant issue. Until recently, the lower classes were often unable to sufficiently feed their families to prevent malnourishment and even starvation (Scheper Hughes 1992: 129–45, 153–63, 207; Goldstein 2003). This atrocious state of affairs has improved considerably as a result of a number of different trends. The first was the introduction of conditional transfer payments to eligible families. These payments were made to families with children to encourage the families to keep their children in school rather than send them out to work. If they meet attendance requirements, the family receives an automatic payment for each child designed to go toward food, medicine, and clothing. Other programs provide assistance for families with different needs. These programs have drastically reduced the prevalence of hunger and malnutrition in Brazil although they have not sufficiently alleviated poverty. The booming economy in Brazil, however, has created new jobs and opportunities and raised a larger proportion of Brazilians into the "middle class."

In the midst of such changes, a proliferation of "haute cuisine" (fine dining) establishments and the associated phenomena of gourmet stores, magazines, TV programs, and cookbooks has raised the bar on how people can set themselves apart from others through refined tastes and consumption. Stores, restaurants, magazines, TV shows, home construction and renovations are all part of a changing landscape. Restaurant culture has long been a part of Brazilian life, particularly among the middle and upper classes who eat out when they cannot return home for lunch or whenever there is no one to cook for them. Even poorer people may consume food cooked by others since they often do not have functioning kitchens, utensils, and so forth, so they buy prepared food from street vendors or small shops. In the past, fine dining often referred primarily to European-style restaurants in the French and Italian tradition. This presumption has changed considerably as Japanese, Chinese, Thai, Portuguese, and even Brazilian restaurants have attained high gastronomic standards and international renown.

In the last several decades, however, restaurants have become global as Brazilians apprentice in Europe and the United States and as Europeans and others move to Brazil and open starred restaurants. Brazilian chefs and restaurants are now part of the international scene and accorded the same honors and status as those that were formerly reserved for a more exclusive community.

Within this landscape, foods and cultures have become reevaluated. A particularly good example of this phenomenon is the way that new chefs showcase ingredients from the Amazon, the *cerrado* and the *mata atlántica*. These items have become valued culinary treats in regions far from their places of origin. Additionally, the foods introduced or used by slave populations or early explorers and foods brought by relatively recent immigrants have risen in the national value system as people look to their own heritages to distinguish themselves from the Euro-American hegemony.

Status and identity take multiple forms in many places, but this truism holds particularly strong in Brazil. Different regions value different forms of music, art, cuisine, dance, recreation and appreciate different body types, house construction, and family relations. The roles played by food, its production, distribution, consumption, and cultural valuation in this complex pattern of social differentiation are the focus of the following chapters, which examine cuisine, identity, value, and social relations in a variety of Brazilian communities.

In Brazil, certain foods take on an iconic status as foods that convey meaning, identity, status, race, class, and gender. In the various chapters of this book I examine

VIGNETTE: CAFÉ DA MANHÃ: STARTING THE DAY

Many Brazilians begin the day with a simple meal of coffee, hot milk, and a roll. This meal is named and conceptualized around the coffee and is often referred to as "drinking" (*tomar*) breakfast. Despite this phrasing, many poor people cannot afford coffee and begin the day with either nothing or a roll. Parents often leave for work before feeding their children. Young children are often left a small sum of money to buy a few rolls from the bakery or local food stall to share among themselves before school.

A working woman, often a domestic worker, will leave home early in the morning to arrive at work in time to prepare *café da manhã* for "her family." She may pick up fresh rolls and perhaps ham and cheese to accompany the rolls. She makes coffee for the family and may also have a cup herself.

After cleaning up the breakfast dishes, she usually shops for the employers' lunch or dinner. In the past, many families ate a large midday meal and those who worked outside the home often came home to eat. Nowadays, this practice is less common since work and home are often long distances apart. If part of the family is home, the domestic will prepare a meal. She may also prepare a dinner/supper to put in the refrigerator that the family can heat up for dinner. She then starts to clean the house or apartment.

The family might choose not to eat at home in the evening. Most cities have a range of restaurant options from very casual *barracas* (stalls), which serve soups or fried fish, to informal family-style restaurants that serve pizzas, steaks, or stews, to fine dining restaurants with a full menu. Restaurants that serve a variety of meats in an all-you-can-eat setting are a Brazilian specialty that will be more fully described later.

Middle-class dining differs from that of the poor in quantity and often in substance too. The poor may share the diet of rice and beans with manioc and pasta but without the fresh greens and meat that the others can afford. The value of *comida farta* is a constant, however.

In some regions of Brazil, breakfast is a more substantial meal, often including porridges made of corn, manioc, wheat, or rice. Often made at home, these dishes are also sold on street corners and markets to passersby. Restaurants and hotels often offer a breakfast buffet that includes coffee, hot milk, fruit, juice, rolls, and specialty rolls like *pão de queijo*, cheese rolls, ham and cheese, and even eggs and frankfurter-like sausages in tomato sauce. This restaurant-style breakfast is found throughout the country.

In certain parts of the country, however, weekend breakfasts may take on a special regional flair. These *cafes da manhã regionais* are found in many rural and semirural areas. Such restaurants, often with pavilion or open-air seating, may offer regional specialties like *açaí* and tapioca, tapioca or corn cakes, sun-dried meat and manioc flour, and numerous other regional dishes. Extended families often gather to enjoy these repasts on their way to shopping or other weekend errands.

a few of the foods and food traditions that instantiate these properties and the social relations and communities that value them. The Afro-Brazilian dishes of the Northeast, the indigenous ingredients of the Amazon, the hearty stews of the European colonists are all embedded in communities that see themselves as the embodiment of their heritage and *terroir*. As was true of Da Matta's daughter, some of these meanings only become evident when they are lost or threatened; others are valued in the repetition of daily life, and this esteem is demonstrated, either in the attention that is given to them or the ubiquitousness of their presence.

Migrations and Flows

Brazil is not only a country of immigration but also a country of internal migration and external emigration. These multiple flows across space and time have impacted the notions of identity and regionality. As a settler colony, Brazil's earliest immigrants were Portuguese explorers and land owners. These early arrivals were often seeking their fortunes and were frequently in motion. They moved among the native populations and often relied on them for food, medicine, and shelter. Without in any way going native, the colonists adapted to new foods like manioc, and *açaí, tucupí, guaraná, cupuaçu, maracujá,* and *pirarucu,* among many others (Camara Cascudo 1983; Radel 2006; Bosisio 2000; Lessa and Meideiros 1999). Early accounts describe not only the pleasure these immigrants took in the local foods (and women) but also the nostalgia (*saudade*) they felt when they returned to Portugal or elsewhere for the land, people, and food.

> The Belem dining table in 1665 was totally indigenous, a permanent feast of roast fish, game and seasonal fruits. Although not yet the fashion, drinking assay [açaí] wine, was a daily and much appreciated habit. Even among the authorities and soldiers few traces remained of Portuguese cuisine, and there were cases of colonial officials returning home who almost died from nostalgia, particularly for the dishes created by the native cuisine. (Souza in Bosisio 2000: 128)

Although most people now see the Amazon region as something of a hinterland, and nowadays the majority of the population lives in the southern regions of Brazil, the earliest arrivals entered along the Amazon River, and Belém was the first capital of Brazil. Foods that are only just now reentering broad popular consumption were then well known and prized by diverse ethnic groups.

As immigration shifted from explorers to settlers, the population moved south, especially along the coast of the Northeast triangle, which became the dominion of sugar barons. The second capital of Brazil was Salvador de Bahia in the heart of the sugar industry. Brazil was the first major producer of sugar plantations and the first to break the monopoly of the sugar trade from the east. As Brazilian plantations came into production, the price of sugar dropped in Europe and the market expanded exponentially. The effects of sugar production on trade and the industrial revolution in Europe and North America have been excellently examined elsewhere (Mintz 1985; Camara Cascudo 1983; Skidmore 2010; Burns 1993), but in Brazil it determined much of the country's early history and economy. Early attempts to recruit labor from the indigenous populations led to a drastic decimation of that population. However traumatic that was for those indigenous groups (*Tupi* and *Guarani* primarily), it was also economically problematic for the local plantation owners who needed enormous manpower to cultivate sugar. In the absence of local labor, they turned to importing slaves from the west of Africa. Over the course of almost three centuries, more than three and a half million Africans were captured and survived the transatlantic voyage to Brazil (Burns 1993: 43). This constituted the largest trade in slaves in history. This huge influx of labor dominated the sugar industry and continues to dominate the culture of much of Brazil.

Although primarily destined for plantations on the northeast coast of Brazil, some slaves were transported to plantations and farming schemes in the Amazon (Nugent and Harris 2004; Acevedo and Ramos de Castro 2004) and others were subjected to the mining of precious metal and gems in the present-day state of Minas Gerais (Burns 1993). Slaves were put to work in all manner of tasks from back-breaking labor in the fields to boiling the cane juice over huge fires, to excavating deep mines, but they were also employed to make sculptures, compose church music, as well as cook, clean, and mind the children for upper-class households (Burns 1993: 45). Pockets of descendant slave populations reside throughout all these regions. Communities of escaped slaves (and some freemen) formed communities called *quilombos* or *mocambos*, which are still dotted across these regions, often in less accessible areas (French 2009).

Descendants of this slave population are today estimated at between 30–50 percent of the total population, but actual figures are hard to verify because census data allows people to self-classify across numerous categories. A number of descendant communities are now documenting their history and status under the *Quilombo* clause in the 1988 Constitution that makes *quilombola* communities eligible for community land reserves (French 2009: xiv). Many of these communities had forgotten or disavowed their heritage and become generic *caboclos*, or mixed-race peasants. Since the 1960s and the civil rights movements in the Unites States, black political and cultural consciousness has expanded tremendously in Brazil as well as elsewhere in the Americas, and there has been a resurgence of local groups searching for their roots (French 2009).

When slavery was finally abolished in Brazil in 1888, most former slaves continued as workers or sharecroppers on plantation and agricultural land, but the economy of Brazil was shifting, first to other agricultural/pastoral pursuits (cattle raising, cacao, coffee farming, rice cultivation, and later soy and wine grapes), and then to more industrial development. The locus of this new activity was south of the sugar belt and as drought and poverty pushed small farmers off their traditional lands and homes, thousands and hundreds of thousands moved to urban and industrial areas looking for better livelihoods. Migrant communities sprang up in most cities, often in shantytowns on the hillsides and peripheries of those urban centers. These shantytowns, now called *favelas*, have proliferated and evolved in every city. Residents of these communities service the homes and businesses of wealthy residents, although some entrepreneurs also began to provide goods and services to *favela* residents. This pattern of rural to urban migration persists today.

The new agricultural ventures also drew migrants from war-torn and poverty-prone areas in Italy, Germany, Japan, Lebanon, and Eastern Europe, among other places. Many of these immigrants settled in ethnic enclaves that still preserve an Old World character a century or more later. Religion, language, dress, music, architecture, and particularly food, mark the distinctive heritage of these groups. Each group has added its own important dishes and ingredients to the national diet, ranging from kibe to sushi to stroganoff. Contemporary migrations from Ukraine, China, Spain, and Portugal increase Brazil's diversity of food and culture.

A few years ago there was an extremely popular *telenovela* called *América* on Globo TV, the most widely watched channel in Brazil.[2] The underlying theme of the series was to "follow your dream," and for many young Brazilians this meant leaving home for better opportunities elsewhere (in a few cases it meant striving to make their dream come true at home). It narrated the story of several individuals in the midst of migrating to big urban areas from the hinterlands and others migrating from urban Brazil to North America. The heroine of the story crosses into the United States from Mexico and lives as an illegal alien in Miami. The glorification of the search for a better destiny became a popular ideal, encapsulated under the title *América*. Several journalists and analysts believed it enticed more people to try to migrate to the United States. Although the journey across the border from Mexico was depicted in gruesome detail, the success of the heroine's venture gave hope to many who currently dream of a migration northward. The movement of peoples from the periphery to the center(s), and the fantasy of the movement northward, demonstrates the mobility of Brazilians both past and present. As Brazilians migrate to the United States, the availability in that country of Brazilian foods like *farinha*, *pão de queijo*, *churrasco*, *guaraná*, and many others increases as groceries and restaurants cater to both an expatriate community and a cohort of foodies into exploring this cuisine.

Another important flow of emigration and migration occurs between Brazil and Portugal. This migration has ebbed and flowed and shifted and reversed numerous times over the past five centuries. The waves of migrants from Portugal to Brazil and from Brazil to Portugal have coincided with the economic destinies of these two countries. Brazilians have privileged access to Portugal, which they have taken advantage of during the prosperous years of the European Union, and Portuguese have flooded the labor markets of Brazil during the latter's times of prosperity. The two nations continue to creatively incorporate elements from the other's culture.

The Portuguese traditions in both food and culture remain an important substrata to Brazilian culture. In particular, Portuguese food traditions ranging from salted cod dishes to seafood stews to cakes and custards heavy with milk, sugar, and butter have influenced many Brazilian food habits. These dishes have been adapted to the ingredients available in Brazil but are recognizably related to those found in Portugal. Portuguese merchants and slave traders traveled around the world conveying people, ingredients, and recipes from one continent to another. All of these flows have influenced Brazilian food and cuisine.

Food and Flows

People travel and food travels and in the process both change and adapt. Food often takes on different meanings and relevance for the community that enjoys it. Sometimes the meaning becomes reified and holds on to a fossilized set of associations and conceptions. Fried polenta in the regions inhabited by central Italian immigrants to Brazil exemplifies this ossification. This dish is ubiquitous in the southern states of Brazil and is served as an appetizer in many homes, restaurants, and community festivals. Polenta was the staple for many immigrants in their home regions of Italy, where it was associated with their hard-scrabble life of scarcity and poverty. Serving it now in immigrant-descended communities commemorates this heritage and a communal sense of shared hardship. Today's elders, however, claim the younger generation has lost appreciation for these meanings of polenta and either view it as boring or as some sort of ethnic stigma attached to the group. Nonetheless, serving the polenta is a continuing tradition. In contrast, *mocotó*, a stew (*guisado*) made of cow's hooves and manioc pieces, is a cartilaginous and sometimes boney concoction that was a staple in both the Northeast and far South of Brazil, both cattle-raising areas, which retains a symbolic value for a range of consumers. This stew instantiates the poverty of the regions and the meager portions of a butchered cow that were affordable to the poorest residents in these regions. Nowadays it is a comfort food to displaced migrants and is served in restaurants in São Paulo and Porto Alegre as a special dish on certain days of the week.

In such ways, foods and their meanings can create a sense of well-being, of place, home, body, and memory for communities of an immigrant diaspora. This sense is constantly renewed and reinforced but its origin may not be consciously recognized. Consciousness surfaces as gaps or absences, changes in availability, cost, and other impediments come into the picture. Sometimes foods take on an iconic status as representing a tradition or a place, but sometimes the sense and value of a food or a dish changes as people move, or as the dish or food becomes available in regions or venues apart from the accustomed areas.

Travel for Food

Culinary tourism has become mainstream. Restaurants, cooking schools, and markets are now standard components if not highlights of the traveler's itinerary. Glossy cookbooks and magazines proliferate in many languages and supplement the standard dining guides. How do we explain this abundant interest in gastronomy? Is culinary tourism a product of affluence, a reflection of a new hedonism, or recognition of the vital role that food plays in all aspects of our social and cultural life? In this mix, several Brazilian foods, and even whole cuisines (such as the foods of Bahia or Minas Gerais), have circulated in an increasingly global society. Brazilian restaurants have opened around the world, so tourists arrive with expectations about the foods they will sample. Enjoyment of these delights becomes a principal way that Brazilians and others overcome the distances between outsiders and themselves. Feeding others and sharing foods are almost universal ways to show solidarity and create good will. Receiving food with respect and enjoyment fosters this relationship and creates a pathway to sharing both substance and meaning. But food plays an important role in drawing distinctions as well. Food is an important marker of identity, and thus is used to emphasize difference as well as similarity.

This book is an examination of the relationship between food, kinship, race, and place in diverse regions in Brazil. I have made no attempt to be inclusive but to pick foods and regions that illustrate the way food exemplifies, creates, and enhances relationships and encounters in daily life. Each chapter focuses on a few dishes and ingredients that form a nexus of meaning rooted in a particular region and examines why certain dishes and ingredients have special salience for food and identity, and speak to issues of race, class, and gender. I examine the contrasts between the ways the foods are appreciated in their home territories with the ways they have come to be used and valued outside the region. In this wider context, many of them have become elements of the emergence of a new food culture in Brazil that is vibrant and creative, and as such, form essential parts of the ongoing transformation of this dynamic nation and its rapidly changing culture.

–2–

Is Bahian *Moqueca* Just Fish Stew?
Food and Identity in Salvador, Bahia

When I first went to Brazil in 1982 as a young wife and mother, we lived for four months in Rio de Janeiro. I became accustomed to the beaches and boulevards, cafes and markets of that beautiful city. After accustoming myself to that Brazil, I was amazed to arrive in Salvador, Bahia, and find a very different atmosphere and culture. In place of the iconic tile sidewalks and tall apartment buildings, Salvador offered cobblestone streets and plazas and colonial architecture. Music, from *samba* to *capoeira* and from Angolan drumming to Yoruba drumming, reverberated through many of the public spaces and drifted through windows, doors, and around street corners. Wafting over all these sensory stimuli was the smell of *dendê* oil and other unfamiliar food scents, mostly prominently emanating from corner stands where Bahian women cooked *acarajé* in pots of the iconic red palm oil boiling over a charcoal fire.[1]

Although I had eaten a Bahian *moqueca* before arriving, I was unprepared for the array of dishes that constituted the regional cuisine nor had I anticipated the pervasive salience Bahian cooking held for the residents of Salvador and the surrounding countryside. Immediately enthralled by this new gustatory experience, I sought to both experience as many dishes as possible and to learn as much as I could about their preparation. My hostess generously shared a few key recipes with me, but being an academically minded person, I sought the written texts as well. My husband and I searched bookstores and restaurants for Bahian cookbooks, but they seemed thin on the ground. We finally found two small collections in Portuguese (Papeta 1979; Junqueira 1977). What made this enterprise even more interesting, and perhaps disconcerting, was the incredulity of my middle-class friends as to why I would want to acquire these books. Why would I want to cook Bahian food? Two things come into perspective in thinking about this cultural dissonance: the first is their wonderment about why I would want to prepare Bahian food; and the second was why I would want to do it myself. In the middle-class Brazilian culture of Rio and São Paulo, if one wanted to eat Bahian food outside of Bahia, one would hire a *Baiana* (Bahian woman) to come to one's home to cook, or one would go to a Bahian restaurant, of which I learned of only one in Rio. Twenty-five years later a new friend gave me a third alternative: one could fly to Bahia. In these conversations I came to realize two things: cooking Bahian food is a manifestation of one's identity as a Bahian, or putting it another way, one has to be Bahian to make this food. The second was an iteration of something I had already experienced but not fully understood, namely that middle-class Brazilians almost never cook for themselves. Leaving the second insight aside for a moment, I want to examine the first.

Bahian Identity

Bahia is a large state in the northeastern part of Brazil. It has a long coastline with numerous bays (*bahias*) and islands along the shore. The interior of Bahia is contiguous with the *sertão* or dry, semiarid region of the Northeast. Bahia was an important sugar-growing area from the 1550s onward and for many years was the richest state (until the discovery of gold in the late seventeenth century). Salvador da Bahia, the principal city in the state, became the capital of Brazil until 1763. The old city and harbor were built during this colonial time and remain classic examples of the colonial architecture. The old section of Salvador was named a UNESCO heritage site in 1985. The center of this district is called the *Pelorinho* after the old pillar that was used to whip and punish unruly citizens and particularly slaves. As the center of the sugar industry, Bahia also became one of the centers of the slave trade. Slave auctions were held in the *Largo do Pelorinho*, the site of the pillory post.

The aftermath of the slave trade remains prominent in the vibrant Afro-Brazilian culture for which Bahia is renowned. This legacy highlights music (*samba*, axe *samba*, reggae *samba*, *capoeira*, Angolan drumming, Yoruba drumming), food, and religion. Activities that had been stigmatized in the context of poverty and racism for their connections to the slave past in the Northeast have, in recent decades, become touted as rich components of a cultural heritage that gives the region a unique identity (Van de Port 2005). In conjunction with this revaluation, the old colonial center of Salvador de Bahia, which had become rundown and impoverished, has been at least superficially refurbished to highlight its charming colonial architecture, plazas, and dramatic views over the harbor. This city and especially the central *Pelorinho* became a destination for tourists both internal and foreign who were drawn by the syncretic blend of music, religion, and local history. One of these magnetic elements is Bahian food, which constitutes a small but distinctive cuisine based on the intersection of foods from Europe, the Americas, and Africa. Although Bahian food has been well known for its distinctive characteristics for a long time, in the last several decades it has emerged as one of the pillars of Bahian identity. Locals repeat the mantra that Bahia is a mixture of indigenous, European, and African cultures, and while this aphorism is true of much of Brazil, it is most strikingly manifest in Bahia, especially in Salvador, and in its distinctive cuisine. Although the food is a well-integrated mixture of indigenous, African, and global ingredients, styles, and

Figure 2.1 *Baiana* in full white attire selling *acarajés* on the beach in Salvador da Bahia. Photograph by Jane Fajans.

techniques, it is best known for its African qualities in large part because it is closely associated with the worship of a pantheon of African deities. These African flavors and the food they create continue to carry their original slave era and diasporic context in the present.

As Bahian identity has increased in prominence, several aspects have taken on iconic status as markers of the region and its culture. Bahian ethnicity and identity became recognizable around the country in the form of a Bahian woman dressed in lacy white clothes of eighteenth-century design. This image is found on tourist posters, magazine and airline advertisements, and in regional guides. Although one can find women clad in this attire in tourist venues in old Salvador, they are also commonly found on street corners or on the beaches throughout the region, cooking and selling *acarajé* dumplings and traditional sweets made from boiled coconut, cocoa, and sugar. These *Baianas* set up their stalls nightly on street corners, on weekend days on the beach, or periodically in the many plazas of the cities during festivals such as the *Festas Juninas* or *Carnaval*.[2] Most *Baianas de acarajé* are attired in turbans, lacey blouses with puffy sleeves, and full skirts with multiple layers. These outfits are mostly white, but can also be in the vibrant colors of West African fabrics. The dress is reminiscent of African market women and the house slaves of the colonial era master's house.

The symbol of the Bahian woman is multivocal. She represents roots, nurture, continuity, and a kind of purity in her appearance and occupation. Part of her

Figure 2.2   *Acarajé* with filling of *vatapá*, shrimp, and peppers. Photograph by Jane Fajans.

symbolic appeal is the purposeful links her attire, her skin color, and her ingredients make to West Africa and the people and food there. This combination highlights her roots with Africa and the food eaten there. Her ability to feed and nurture others with scant resources is associated with female values of the wife and mother. What makes her visual appeal most arresting, however, is her ability to maintain an unblemished frilly white outfit on an urban street corner while deep frying dumplings in hot and sputtering red oil. She is thus a symbol of an idealized wife and mother spanning past and present.

Acarajés, which are Bahian dumplings, are made of black-eyed peas soaked and pounded or blended into a paste. This is then made into a ball and deep fried. The dumpling is served hot, split in half, and filled with *vatapá* (a kind of bread pudding made with soaked stale bread, nuts, and *dendê* oil) and topped with dried shrimp and a hot pepper sauce. The *acarajé* is eaten in one's hands, with the *vatapá* and other condiments spilling and dripping over the sides, making this a fitting food for outdoor eating. This dumpling and the red palm oil in which it is fried are both derived from West African Yoruba cuisine. Beyond its African-ness (Hamilton 2001), this dumpling incorporates the abundant seafood caught off Bahia's miles of coastline, the European flavors of bread and wheat, and native crops like cashews and pimentos. This dish thus incorporates ingredients from the various flows that have converged upon Bahia. Although messy to eat, this whole dish is portable and can be eaten as you walk or loll in your beach chair. It encapsulates Bahia.

As I mentioned above, the quintessential symbol of Bahia is a *Baiana* woman selling *acarajé* and *doces* (coconut sweets) on a street corner. These foods are only a few of a number of street foods sold on the plazas and beaches of Brazil. Street food is very popular in Brazil and people, often whole families, promenade in the evenings to snack. On the weekends, they may spend hours on the beach. During these outings, they can sample a variety of foods such as shrimp, cashews, grilled cheese, popsicles, coconuts, popcorn, soft drinks, beer, and *acarajé*. Many of these snacks are sold by perambulating vendors who snake through the crowds selling their wares, but small beachside stalls also set out tables and beach chairs that families appropriate for hours, intermittently ordering beer or a snack while also buying from the itinerant vendors and *acarajé* sellers who set up near these beach-front establishments. The informality of beach culture, including the lack of clothing, which makes Brazil (in)famous in the Euro-American imagination, contrasts greatly with the old-fashioned formality of the *Baiana* cook. She sits among these scantily clad people in her full skirt, turban, and lace top, like an anchor to the past, a representative of what has transformed in today's society of leisure and relative plenty. She is a symbol of what is particularly Bahian in the midst of the more generic Brazilian pastimes of the beach and carnival.

São Joaquim Market

While the *Baiana* is the public face of Bahia, behind the scenes there is a less elegant and less pristine side to Salvadorian cuisine. *São Joaquim* Market in Salvador is a vibrant and fascinating place. *São Joaquim* is neither a street market nor a designated municipal plaza filled with market stalls. Rather, the market is a warren of streets and alleys in which some stands open into small store-like spaces and others are just stalls set up in the middle or sides of the alley. *São Joaquim* is a permanent market that has grown and folded into itself over the many decades of its existence. Although there are sections of the market that specialize in certain foods, meats, beans, flours, fish, live chickens and ducks, and cooking pots, this order is not totally consistent and different types of foods coexist haphazardly with *Candomblé* (Afro-Brazilian religion prevalent particularly in the Northeast) artifacts, tropical birds, soaps, and utensils. On the fringes of the densest part of the market are small corrals where goats and chickens are kept until needed. Although some of these animals are there to be butchered and sold in the stalls, many are bought live and taken to the *Candomblé terreiros* for ritual sacrifices.

This bustling and frenetic place is the heart of food culture in Salvador, but until recently was off the beaten track for tourists and outsiders. In an attempt to change this, and coincidently underscore the African heritage of the community, in 2006, the Prefecture sponsored a photo exhibit in the market itself. The photographs constituting the exhibit, *Lá e Cá* ("Here and There"), were hung on lighted boxes throughout

Figure 2.3 A stall selling beans, rice, dried shrimp, and *dendê* oil in the *São Joaquim* Market in Salvador. Photograph by Jane Fajans.

the market, suspended over the aisles, tucked in the corner of an open stall, on the wall of a building, and any other nook that could possibly take a photo. Given the visual confusion of the market with its laden counters, stacked shelves, and various meats, lanterns, hooks, ropes, baskets, pots, and other goods hanging from overhead beams, this was not an ideal venue for a photo display. It was hard to know if one had actually perused the entire exhibit since the pictures were essentially camouflaged and there were so many other visual stimuli in the market. This exhibit certainly made more people aware of the market (it was advertised in newspapers, brochures, and on the sides of buses) but I did not notice much difference in the clients actually strolling around the market.

The photos were taken in and around Angola, Africa, and Salvador, Brazil, both *Lá e Cá*, "Here and There," as the exhibit title connotes. The implicit theme of the exhibit stressed the similarities between the two historically connected regions. The photos portrayed children playing, women cooking, portraits of old and young, female and male, streets with people and animals, and market stalls with bottles of *dendê* oil and piles of ceramic pots. None of the pictures had labels or designations on them indicating in which country they were taken.[3] No one I spoke to claimed they could tell which picture had been taken in which place, and I certainly did not have any grounds for distinguishing them. It seemed a matter of pride to many of the Brazilians I spoke with that they could not tell the origin of one photo or another. This exhibit had the effect of making visual what had been strongly believed and valued already: Bahia retains much of its African heritage. On one level, however, the exhibit objectified the people and settings it portrayed by decontextualizing them; but on another level, it powerfully conveyed the feeling of a shared identity that transcended different contexts (and different continents).

Near the *São Joaquim* Market is a municipal fish market. This market is markedly and immediately different from the bustling and undisciplined activity of the *Feira de São Joaquim*. Here, in a new and tiled building with a ceiling two stories high, fish vendors sell their wares in neat cubicles. The fish are kept in refrigerators or on trays of ice, and counters and scales are clean and clear. Many of the stalls have prepackaged containers of cut-up seafoods ready to be used for *moqueca* or *bobó*, two of the signature Bahian dishes. These plastic bags have layers of shelled mussels, shrimp, crab, and fish ready to be marinated in lime and simmered in a wok-shaped *moqueca* pot for a *moqueca* or *bobó* meal. Shoppers do not need to choose or weigh their selections; they just pick a bag of the appropriate size. To make the dish even easier to prepare, a small stall containing crates of tomatoes, peppers, limes, coconuts, and cilantro, the principal ingredients for *moqueca*, stands near the market entrance. This stall provided the only nonmarine products available in this market. Assuming a household has *dendê*, rice, and coconut milk at home, a busy cook could drop by here and in one stop pick up the wherewithal for the evening or weekend meal. In contrast to the *Feira de São Joaquim*, this market was practically empty when I visited it.

Home Cooking

Food in Bahia is a family affair. Discussions around food focus on who made it, what was served, and who was there to eat it. Family meals, especially family gatherings, are important and frequent, and many extended families gather for a weekly meal. Friends like to describe the different meals that their families enjoyed on weekends. One man described how he cooked on Saturday mornings and made *bobó de camarões* (a shrimp and manioc dish), which he presented to his extended family at mid-day. Another described how his family gathered every Sunday for *cozido* (a meat and vegetable stew). Most families gather on Saturday, but this latter informant's family accommodated the schedule of one son who took courses on Saturday so they postponed their weekly meal until Sunday. Holding family gatherings on Sunday, instead of Saturday, is not an uncommon practice in response to scheduling conflicts. The family get-together, as well as the food consumed, creates a comfort zone of familiarity and satisfaction. Along with the popular *cozido* (meat and vegetable stew), *bobó de camarões* (mashed manioc with shrimp and *dendê* oil), and *moqueca*, one finds family celebrants eating other dishes like *frango com molho pardo* (chicken with a dark sauce of chicken's blood) and *abobora com camarões* (pumpkin stuffed with shrimp). Of the dishes mentioned above, *bobó de camarões* is the most popular meal at these sorts of gatherings. *Bobó de camarões* is a polenta-like mush, although made of manioc instead of corn, with shrimp, vegetables, and *dendê* oil. It is a filling (*farta*) comfort food.

Bobó de Camarão

Ingredients

2 lbs. of fresh shrimp
2 lbs. of manioc (can be bought frozen in many stores)
1 onion
4 sprigs of cilantro
2 cloves of garlic
1 tomato
Salt to taste
½ cup of *dendê* oil (available outside of Brazil online, or in specialty stores)
1½ cups of coconut milk

Preparation

1. Cook the manioc until soft like a potato.
2. Make a *moqueca* with the shrimp and tomatoes (see recipe on following pages).
3. Beat the manioc with the coconut milk.
4. Stir in the *moqueca*.

Outsiders associate Bahian food with the *Baiana*, and see it as produced by a female-gendered body. In particular, cooking for the *orixás* is done by the women adepts of the *terreiros* (see next section). Inside Bahia most household cooks are women and cooking is still a feminine activity; however, many men are proud of their cooking skills and enjoy cooking for their families. Since Bahian food is such an important part of Bahian identity, the ability to prepare this food and offer it to others is one many Bahians, including men, seek to share. Cooking and eating are equally valued activities and can be done by both genders, although women are usually the public face of the cuisine.

As in other parts of the world where food is so embedded in the meaning and rhythm of everyday life, Bahian food is seen as enmeshed in the fabric of family and religion. It combines and recombines a number of ingredients, including dried shrimp, seafood of all kinds, tomatoes, onions, peppers, cilantro, manioc, cashews, coconut milk, and *dendê* oil. There are countless variations on the dishes. Modes of preparation are passed down between generations and among friends. Each family prides itself on its own variation, which they consider the best.

More Than Just a Good Meal: *Candomblé* and Feeding the *Orixás*

Bahian food exists to feed an other worldly realm in addition to the local and foreign inhabitants of this earthly one. Behind the public presence of the *Baiana* is the world of *Candomblé*, the Afro-Brazilian religion practiced widely across the nation but closely associated with the African slaves brought to the Northeast sugar-producing regions. *Baianas* also feed the deities of the *Candomblé* pantheon. Female members of the *terreiros* (religious houses) continue to dress in outfits inspired by African and eighteenth-century colonial styles. As adepts in these religious houses, they honor the deities, *orixás*, by preparing ritual foods for each one on special occasions. Each *orixá* is associated with a particular food, a fruit, a drink, a color, a day of the week or month, and an environmental niche. Many people in Bahia wear white on Fridays, to show their respect for *Oxalá*, the god of creation who has become associated with that color and that day. *Acarajés* are ritually important as the food of a *Candomblé* deity named *Yansá* (*Iansá*). Adepts feed her this food once a month on Wednesday, which is her day.[4] *Xangô* is fed *caruru*, an okra dish, and *Oxum* is given *ximxim de galinha*, a chicken stew, as well as *moqueca*. *Moqueca* is also offered to *Yemanjá*, the goddess of the sea (Ribeiro 1962; Radel 2006).

Some of these foods have also come to be associated with Catholic saints through their association with particular African deities. Syncretistic cults like *Candomblé* are products of the mixture of African and Catholic religions, and the long history of repression of African cultures in the New World. Each god in *Candomblé* is associated with a saint in the Catholic Church, although the actual saint associated with an *orixá* may vary from region to region or *terreiro* to *terreiro* (Ribeiro 1962). Feast days intended to celebrate particular African gods, the *orixás*, were simultaneously associated with certain Catholic saints such as *São Cosme* or *São Damião*, *Santa Barbara*, the Virgin Mary, and many others who came to stand in for a different *orixá* and provide occasions for worship that were acceptable to the dominant society. In such cases, Bahians may prepare an honorific and festive meal dedicated to a Catholic saint too.

One such ritual meal is *caruru*. Ordinary *caruru* is a vegetable dish made with okra, and is called *caruru só* (only *caruru*). If you invite someone to a *caruru festa*, however, the guests expect a ritual meal of *ximxim de galinha*, *vatapá*, *acarajé*, *caruru*, *farofa*, *efó*, *milho branco*, yams, beans, and *pipoca*.[5] This meal is prepared for the deity *Xangô* and on saints' days like those of *São Cosme* and *São Damião*[6] or for a festival like the second of February, the day of the sea goddess, *Yemanjá*, or for less formal celebrations like a birthday or family reunion (Ribeiro 1962). Individuals occasionally plead with a saint or *orixá* to grant a request for health, love, prosperity, or other personal desires, vowing to provide such a feast if the wish comes to be. The fulfillment of such a vow provides food and faith for a community of adherents.

An important aspect of the *Candomblé* religion is animal sacrifice. Goats and chickens are the most commonly sacrificed animals. This ritual practice was made very apparent on one of my visits to the public market of Salvador, *São Joaquim*, where I came close to being run over by a wheelbarrow trundling a goat out of the market, bound for sacrificial rendezvous with the deity.

Two *Moquecas*

If there is one signature ingredient in Bahian cooking that embodies the culture, heritage, and identity of the place and people, it is *azeite de dendê*, *dendê* oil. This oil is pressed from the pulp, not the kernel, of the red palm tree (Elaeis *guinensis*), which is native to West Africa and is orange-red in color. Although high in antioxidants, it is also high in saturated fat, which has made it less popular with cholesterol-conscious consumers. Although still an essential ingredient in Bahian food, it is no longer used in as great quantities as it once was. Except in the case of *acarajé*, *dendê* oil is not usually used as a basic cooking oil, but as a flavoring, usually added shortly before finishing a dish. It gives a tangy flavor and a slightly viscous texture to any dish to which it is added.

In Bahia, most locals do not know that other regions produce *moquecas*, *vatapás*, and *carurus* too. They think of these dishes as local specialties unique to the Bahian (or at least Northeast) region, and as a product of the ethnic confluence of Portuguese, African, and Brazilian indigenous influences. Bahians were surprised to hear that I had eaten *moquecas* in Espirito Santo (a state just to the south of Bahia) and *vatapás* in Pará. In particular, they were aghast to learn that Espirito Santo claimed superiority in the art of making *moqueca*. Outside of Bahia, however, the *moqueca*s of Espirito Santo are well known and touted by the *cognoscenti*. I was first told of them by acquaintances from Rio and planned a visit to Espirito Santo on their recommendation. In Espirito Santo the competition between the two regions is best expressed by the saying "*Moqueca é so Capixaba[7] o resto é peixada*" ("The only *moqueca* is *Capixaba*, the rest is only fish stew"), a saying flaunted on posters throughout the capital of Espirito Santo, Vitória.

This culinary competition pits the old Afro-Brazilian state of Bahia (and by extension other Northeast states) against the more European-influenced state of Espirito Santo. The travel literature on Espirito Santo emphasizes the Swiss-like farms and woodland scenery of the interior where wine and cheese production are important industries. While both *moqueca*s are delicious, the Espirito Santo *moqueca* is actually the dish more akin to ordinary Brazilian fish stew (*peixada*) in its ingredients and the way they are prepared. The Bahian *moqueca* is a distinctly different sort of dish. Bahian *moqueca* is made from seafood, shrimp, crab, mussels, fish, and/or a combination of the above. These ingredients are marinated in a ceviche-like lime, hot pepper, and cilantro mixture and cooked in coconut milk and *dendê*, which as noted above, was originally brought from Africa. The result is a creamy distinct flavor with a bit of a bite. The *moqueca* is served with rice and a polenta-like porridge (*pirão*) made with manioc flour and *dendê*. Bahian food, which is based on *dendê* oil, is very distinctive. The ingredients that go into Bahian food are self-consciously understood by the Bahians as representing their cultural/ethnic mix of European, African, and indigenous cultures (the manioc flour is recognized as indigenous).

Figure 2.4 *Moqueca Baiana* with *pirão*, rice, and *farinha* in a typical presentation. Photograph by Jane Fajans.

Seafood *Moqueca* (*Moqueca Mariscara*) from Bahia
For 6–8 people

Ingredients

1 lb. of fresh shrimp or prawns

1 lb. of meaty fish fillet (scrod, sea bass, monk fish, etc.)

1 lb. of squid (optional)

2 lbs. of mussels or crab legs (to garnish the top)

1 bunch of cilantro

2–3 tomatoes

1 green pepper

1 sweet white or red onion

1–3 chili peppers (by taste)

2–4 limes

½ cup of good olive oil

1–2 cups of coconut milk (or one 14-oz. can)

Salt

½ cup of *dendê* oil

Preparation

1. Smash or chop ½ of the cilantro with salt. Mix with the juice of the limes, and diced chili pepper.

2. Marinate the fish and squid in the lime, cilantro, and pepper mixture for at least ½ hour.
3. Slice the onion, pepper, and tomatoes in rings.
4. Arrange layers of vegetables in a pot. Bahians use a red clay pot shaped like a wok, so a wok is a reasonable substitute.
5. Add olive oil and turn the heat on medium-low.
6. When vegetables begin to cook and oil is hot, add fish, squid, and coconut milk.
7. When the fish is almost done, add shrimp and mussels or crabs to the top of the dish and drizzle *dendê* oil over the top.
8. Cook until shrimp are pink and oil is "cooked."
9. Garnish with cilantro.
10. Serve with plain rice and *pirão* if desired.

The *Capixaba moqueca*, in contrast, does not include coconut milk or red palm oil, and instead uses *urucú* (annatto or *colorão*) and tomato to give a red color to the stew. The fish and vegetables (tomato, onion, cilantro, and garlic) are cooked together in a fish stock (Santos Neves and Pacheco 2002: 104, 107). The result closely resembles the fish stews of Mediterranean Europe.

*Capixaba*s (people from Espirito Santo) say that their *moqueca* is purer and that a good fish stew does not need the extra flavors of coconut milk and *dendê*.

Moqueca Capixaba

Ingredients

2 lbs. of fish (*badejo*) in cutlets
1 lb. of diced tomatoes
1 lb. of diced onions
1 bunch of cilantro
2–3 spring onions
2 cloves of chopped garlic
½ cup of olive oil
¼ cup of annatto
2 limes
Salt to taste
1 cup of fish stock

Preparation

1. Heat the olive oil in an earthenware pan and brown the onion lightly.
2. Add half the diced tomato and onion.
3. Season the fish cutlets with salt and lemon and place in the pan.
4. Cover the fish with the rest of the tomato and onion.

5. Add the coriander, salt, annatto, and stock.
6. Allow to cook for about 10–15 minutes without stirring.
7. Check to see if the fish is cooked and with sufficient salt.
8. Add a few drops of lemon juice. (Santos Neves and Pacheco 2002: 35)

For *Capixabas* the extra flavorings (*tempero*) of Bahian *moqueca* are excessive (Eze-kial 2006), and they claim their *moqueca* is simple and pure. But what is this simplic-ity and purity? It is essentially the absence of African ingredients, not the absence of flavorings per se. Without saying it, but with an implicit meaning, the *Capixaba* *moqueca* advertises itself as a white, purely European, dish, more like the seafood dishes of Portugal or France. There is, thus, a racist undertone to the culinary competition. In effect, the *Capixaba* are saying, "We have no African heritage and thus we make a purer *moqueca*."[8] The Bahians, by contrast, say their *moqueca* is a unique dish that stands apart from virtually all other fish dishes because of the signa-ture combination of ingredients. The competition between Espirito Santo and Bahia over *moqueca* versus fish stew is also a way of marking the differences between the two states and their people. Espirito Santo is whiter, richer, and more European in outlook. This signals inclusive and exclusive categories of race and class, of differ-ence, purity and exoticism. Because *moqueca* has become such an important part of Bahian identity, Bahians presume it is a Bahian dish. The *Capixabas* are trying to

Figure 2.5 *Moqueca Capixaba*, often served with *pirão* as well. Photograph by Jane Fajans.

undermine this presumption and prove themselves superior in the culinary domain. They actively promote their cuisine as a tourist attraction and as a symbol of their distinctive identity.

But how is it that Espirito Santo focuses on this competition while Bahia does not even seem to be aware of it? Herein lies the power of identity politics. Although poor and until recently economically underdeveloped, Bahia has preserved a strong regional identity and presence in the national and international arenas. Bahian music, religion, and food are markers of place and community. In the past, and frequently in Brazil today, people have a hard time conceiving of Bahian food outside of Bahia, and even if it is prepared outside of Bahia, they imagine it must be prepared by a *Baiana* (Bahian woman). For Bahians the foods constituting their essence are not just recipes: they are the residue of a history and a unique regional and cultural identity of which they are proud. Eating certain foods can make you Bahian, and food is Bahian because of where and by whom it is cooked. You are what you eat, but you also make/cook what you are. For this reason, Bahian food is intrinsically associated with those whose essence it embodies.

Espirito Santo does not seem to have such a definite identity, and it is not generally seen as an interesting tourist destination, either inside or outside of Brazil. Food and foodways do not immediately differentiate a *Capixaba* from anyone else in Brazil except Bahians. Instead the immigrants who settled there and their descendants who now live there are of European extraction. Espirito Santo has a much smaller Afro-Brazilian population than Bahia.

Interestingly, according to my personal, nonrandom, and unscientific sample of (non-Bahian) Brazilians I encountered and worked with, when middle- or upper-class Brazilians from other regions attempt to make *moqueca* or order it at restaurant, they tend to prefer the *Capixaba* to the Bahian variety. Many claim that the *dendê* oil is too heavy or unhealthy. They seem to feel more comfortable with the "purer," less African, more familiar version. These preferences are hard to express in overt cultural terms. They cannot talk about people in terms of difference or purity so this sense of social and cultural difference is imputed to a taste difference. The race and class differences are masked by displacing them onto an external object, a fish stew, which takes on symbolic importance beyond its substance. Food is identity and identity is food. For this reason, *moqueca* can never be just fish stew.

Embodied to Disembodied, Inalienable to Alienable: Bahian Food Becomes Global

Brazilians see Bahian food as inextricable from the body of a Bahian who both produces it and is produced by it. Bahians are open to sharing both their food and culture. They are particularly pleased to teach others to prepare their signature dishes, and although they are not as prevalent as in some parts of the world, there is an increasing number of cooking classes and cookbooks, in Salvador, the capital of Bahia. The language schools of Bahia typically offer a trinity of extracurricular classes that includes cooking, *capoeira,*[9] and *samba.* I took the cooking and *samba* classes.

Although distinctive in flavor, Bahian dishes are relatively simple to make. As I mentioned above, when I first went to Bahia in 1982, I became enamored with the food and wanted to prepare it myself. My search for a regional cookbook finally netted two small collections of recipes (Papeta 1979; Radel 2005). These collections were just slightly fancier than mimeographed collections such as those put out by clubs or associations in the United States, and they have fallen into pieces with the years of use I have given them. On more recent trips over the past few years, I have noticed a florescence of glossy cookbooks with fabulous color photos and expanded discussions of the role of food in the regional cuisines of Brazil (Dos Santos 2005; Radel 2005, 2006). These new books are very much oriented toward a tourist market, and they have full translations in English and more extended discussions of the ingredients employed. Cookbooks symbolize several processes of identity building (Appadurai 1988). They signify a collection of dishes that can be labeled as belonging to a group: regional, national, religious, community, ethnicity, and so forth. They also betoken a change in the attitude people have toward their cuisine. A cuisine that can be represented in a book is alienable. It is no longer something that comes into being through activity alone, it exists as an abstraction beyond any particular manifestation of it. Recipes are no longer things that reside in people's heads and hands. They can be detached and exchanged with others, taught in the aforementioned cooking classes, and laid out in print and photos. Such a cuisine is no longer embodied in particular subjects or understood as an extension of that subject's relations with the world.

I believe Bahian food was, and still is thought of, to some extent, as inalienable. Cooking it is still assumed to be an embodied practice that one can only do if it is a part of one's socialization. This is why Brazilians from outside Bahia and the Northeast assume that if you want Bahian food, you must hire a *Baiana/o* to make it. The commodification of this cuisine through cookbooks and restaurants is aimed at an audience primarily beyond Brazil who see the food as less embedded and embodied in a regional identity, and as alienable from their religious, social, and regional connections. For these reasons, the lovely and expensive books have English and Spanish translations.

The Indigenous Side of Bahian Food

Although the popular conception of Bahian food focuses on its African ingredients, many of its ingredients are indigenous to the Americas. Of the nonmarine ingredients in *moqueca,* tomatoes, pepper, and the manioc meal mush (*pirão*) are all native

American foods (Foster and Cordell 1992). In Bahia, and especially in Salvador, the most common description I heard was that Bahia was a region in which Portuguese, African, and indigenous cultures came together. This confluence is recognized in several domains. Socially, the confluence emerges in the variety of mixed-race people throughout the state. This mixture is further evidenced during syncretic rituals such as those that constitute *Candomblé*. When participants of this ritual go into trance, I was told during such an occasion, they can be possessed by one of two types of spirits: an African spirit or a *caboclo* spirit. The *caboclo* is a person of mixed-race (Brazilian or Afro-Brazilian and Indian). The different types of spirits have different personalities; the *caboclos* are more serious while the Africans are "happier" and imbibe a great deal of alcohol while in trance. The same person can be possessed by both spirits (at different moments) and onlookers observe their behavior to judge which spirit has taken possession.

The interweaving of the various ethnicities is also present in the language, where words like *orixá*, *Candomblé*, and *acarajé* are part of the daily language in the Northeast and are not commonly spoken in the rest of Brazil. A parallel case, considered in a later chapter, is the influx of Amazonian Indian words in the daily language of the northern region, of which Bahia is only one part.

Festas Juninas

Although distinctive in many ways that I have been attempting to describe, Bahia shares many traits with other Northeastern states and to some extent with the rest of Brazil. The rural, inland region of Bahia with its rituals and foods is essentially continuous with this distinctive regional culture. The shared continuities are evident in another important Brazilian festival. This celebration lasts for almost a month and is called the *Festas Juninas* (June Festivals). This series of festivities is celebrated throughout the country, especially in rural areas. The description that follows here is applicable to many parts of Brazil, but the emphasis on certain foods is of particular significance in the interior of Bahia and throughout the Northeast since indigenous food is consciously described as playing a very important role. Aspects of the festival are celebrated almost nightly from June 13, the day of Saint Anthony (the patron saint of lovers: thus this day is celebrated as Brazil's Valentine's Day), to the day of Saint Peter on June 29. The largest celebrations occur on the eve of June 24, which is celebrated for the festival of *São João* (St. John). This saint's day occurs around the solstice. It has long been celebrated in Europe as a mid-summer festival. In Brazil, of course, it is a "mid-winter" celebration, although winter is a relative term in most of the country. This festival occurs across the country, but in Bahia it is associated with the interior part of the state, which is the traditional agricultural area. People head into the interior for a twenty-four- to seventy-two-hour period of all-night music, dancing, and eating. *São João* is a family-and-friends gathering, a return to the *pequena cidade* ("small town") one or one's family hailed from before migrating to the cities. During this period, many urban dwellers reverse the migrations of the last half century and return to their rural communities. The roads and bus stations are mobbed as the city folk head back to small towns and farms. Here they celebrate with local music, dance, and food, and big bonfires that light up the short(est) days of the year. Of course, much of the "folklore" aspect of the folk festival has become increasingly commercialized and many of the music groups performing are contemporary music bands.

Some interior cities and towns now promote *São João* parties in June. They put on shows and dance competitions, and host *quadrilhas* ("square dancing") for the general public. One such destination is Cruz das Almas, a town on the west side of the Recôncavo (the area around the Bay of All Saints, *Bahia de Tudos Santos*) about 150 kilometers from Salvador. Cruz das Almas now has a big fairground with multiple stages for alternating and/or competing bands, a big open area for dancing, and a ring of booths with tables for participants to sit, eat, and drink. The residential streets are lined with log piles ready to be lit to celebrate the saint's day. Cruz das Almas became famous because of the local homemade firecrackers called *espetos*, which men and boys (seemingly many fewer women) set off in the streets, aimed not at the sky but zigzagging about two feet above the street and frequently (or at least sometimes) coming into contact with friends or foes. The atmosphere is charged with energy and loud noises. It was not a scene that I particularly enjoyed.

The music and dancing during this festival is more "folkloric" than the popular music and *samba* traditions of the urban areas and festivals like *Carnaval*. This holiday is more reminiscent of European traditions than African ones. The main instruments are the guitar, *zambumba* (triangle), and accordion. The principal dance is the *forró*, a basic two-step that is credited to early English sailors who traveled between coastal cities.

Foods play an important role in this month-long series of festivals. In particular, corn is a signature food and is served in multiple forms. Corn is another important indigenous food of the Americas, and plays an important historic as well as social role. Important to the indigenous populations, corn plays a role in the mythology of a great number of different tribes (see Chapter 3). Many of these groups have a ritual, the New Corn Ceremony, which is found in different forms in different indigenous groups. Corn is eaten roasted, boiled, steamed, as a porridge, in cakes, and as a dough or *masa*. The June festivals coincide with the corn harvest and feature a wide variety of different corn dishes. More significantly, the corn dishes feature prominently in people's minds when they think of this time of year. Friend after friend mentioned that my interest in food would be captivated by the myriad corn dishes available at these events, and they would lovingly count off the different foods such as *pamonha*, *mingau*, *angu*, *puba*, *pipoca*, and cakes made with cornmeal and flour. They led me to believe that corn and only corn was the core of the festival, an exaggeration as I later realized. Nonetheless, there are many corn dishes, and many special foods associated with this holiday. I have a food magazine devoted to foods for the *Festas Juninas*, which has more than thirty different corn dish recipes (Kernbeis 2007).

The identification of the June Festivals with the countryside and agricultural regions is underscored by a theatrical performance of a shotgun wedding. This skit is performed all over the country by schoolchildren dressed in *caipira* ("hillbilly") clothing. In this short enactment, a pregnant woman is dragged by her father, who carries a shotgun, before a priest who marries her to the father of her child. All the men/boys in the play wear straw hats, bandanas, and checkered shirts to signify their *caipira* identity. The girls (other than the bride who wears white) wear gingham skirts, shawls, pigtails, and have round circles of rouge painted on their cheeks and a layer of freckles dotted on top. This totally stereotypic enactment is performed in schools, in shopping centers, in plazas, even in airport check-in areas, and on stages across the country.

A second tradition in the North and Northeast are the dance competitions in which schoolchildren and clubs of adolescents and adults perform *quadrilhas*, originally a form of square dance (*quadrilha* means square). Today these dances are highly choreographed performances in squares and lines facing the judging stand. The groups consist of twenty to forty performers who rehearse for months.[10] The female dancers wear colorful ruffled skirts and shawls a good deal more revealing than the stereotypic costume of the children dressed as *caipiras*, while the men wear white shirts and trousers with straw hats. These dances are energetic and boisterous and greatly cheered by large audiences, often filled with the group's supporters who may try to shout down the supporters of the rival groups.

In Bahia many people return to the countryside to celebrate this holiday. At this festival much of the food is actually made of corn: corn fritters, corn cakes, cornbread, corn porridge, corn on the cob, sweetened corn mash steamed in corn husks (*pamonha*), or popcorn. One food, popcorn, has taken on a symbolic meaning and use different from that which it has in other parts of the world. Popcorn in the United States and Europe is a snack food closely associated with children and entertainment, the most common food eaten while watching a movie. It is used in similar ways in Bahia as well, sold on the streets and in movie theaters. But it has additional properties associated with *Candomblé*. During a ritual for *Omulú*, who is often associated with Saint Lazarus, the ground of the church square of the Saint Lazarus Church is covered in popcorn, which people rub on their own bodies to protect themselves against contagious diseases (Lewis 1992). In addition to being used in rituals, popcorn, *pipoca*, is a term used in Salvador to describe a person who hangs out on the streets, especially during *Carnaval*. The *pipoca* does not pay to participate in any of the more formal *Carnaval* activities, such as joining a *bloco*[11] or watching the events from the luxury of a *camarote*, which is a balcony overlooking the street. Rather, he or she jumps from one activity to another like popcorn when it is being popped.

São João is a harvest festival, and as a family celebration, it feels a lot more like Christmas than Brazil's "real" Christmas (or *Natal*), which occurs in mid-summer.

The immediate association between this food and this festival stems from the fact that corn is the main staple of the interior; the abundance of corn dishes is a celebration of the region's bounty and coincides with the corn harvest. These corn-based foods are accompanied by bonfires, firecrackers, and *licor de genipapo* (a sweet liquor made from the black juice of the genipapo fruit) (Anon. 2012a). Nowadays, however, beer is as omnipresent as *genipapo* liquor, and other drinks made of *cachaça* and fruit appear as well. Both corn and genipapo plants are native to the Americas, and both have been extensively used by the indigenous population. Genipapo is not just a food. Its juice is also commonly used by indigenous peoples to paint black designs on their bodies. As a distilled liquor, it transcends its indigenous use and combines native ingredients with Western techniques of alcohol production. In this way it represents an amalgam of Indian, black, and white symbols.

Beyond this rather obvious connection of bounty and harvest, however, lies the association of corn with the culinary exchange that occurred when Portuguese, Africans, and Native Americans converged. Corn or maize has been an important crop throughout the Americas. In much of Brazil, corn does not currently constitute a major part of the diet, that role being taken by rice and beans or manioc. Nevertheless, corn retains its association with its indigenous origins and can symbolize the ritual that celebrates people's return to their roots, to their homes in the interior from which they or their ancestors migrated, to the agricultural lifestyle that is far from the quotidian experience of the urban dweller, and to a less sophisticated time when whole families celebrated holidays together.

Although the history of these food and ritual relations is obscure, the colonial powers of Spain and Portugal introduced the saint's day celebrations of Saint Anthony, Saint John, and Saint Peter to the New World. They also demanded tribute from the *latifundos* (large landowners) and their workers, which at this time of year was paid in corn, especially in the early days before the sugar plantations became fully installed. In other Latin American countries (e.g., former colonies of Spain such as Colombia, Peru, Ecuador, and Bolivia), Saint John's Day was also the time that peasants had to pay their annual tribute to the crown (Roldan 2009). Much of the tribute was offered in agricultural produce, particularly corn, so corn is closely associated with this event and with the gathering of large numbers of people to celebrate this bountiful time of year. The events became paired and the festivals celebrated both the saints and the harvest.

As people migrate from the rural areas of the interior to urban ones, aspects of their culture move too. Foods are frequently carried from one region to another, and while they can continue to be enjoyed in their new setting, the meanings they embody may change in the transition. When these foods get exported to other regions, these associations may be attenuated or lost entirely. As mentioned above, *caruru* is made for certain occasions in Bahia. In Pará, however, *caruru* is not part of a religious calendar or invested with ritual potency. It is simply a delicious dish that accompanies other dishes as a component of Pará's regional cuisine. We cannot completely trace the changes that have occurred over the centuries that different foods have been prepared in Brazil, but we can look at the differences that have evolved in different regions to help highlight the value of these culinary symbols. One major change is how *caruru* and *vatapá* came to be made without *dendê* oil as they traveled north with migrating workers. This absence gives these dishes a very different taste and a somewhat different texture. As in the contrast between Bahian and *Capixaba moqueca*, the absence of these ingredients may also tacitly give them different associations of racial and subcultural identity.

—3—

Pará's Amazonian Identity: Manioc Six Ways

The Amazon's famed biodiversity comes alive in the colorful sights and pungent scents of the aisles and stalls of the plentiful Amazonian markets. The array of fruits and vegetables, plants and fish, nuts and berries, all sourced from the region astounds in the enormity of seasonal variability. Despite this abundance, the Amazon is not particularly noted for its cuisine. Most people do not think of the Amazon region as one which is "culture-rich" with long histories of different cultural influences, although this is, in fact, the case. Instead the Amazon evokes the wonders of nature in its most exotic, raw, and inaccessible form. As a vast region stretching across parts of seven Brazilian states and six South American countries, the Amazon retains an aura of the wild frontier despite considerable development in the area.

In accord with this perception, outsiders do not think of the Amazon as a region with a culinary or gastronomic tradition. Why is this? One probable reason is that the cuisines of the region are based on indigenous ingredients and modes of preparation. This is not to say that they are "indigenous" dishes, but that many of the ingredients are indigenous and some of the modes of preparation retain indigenous methods. Certainly these dishes have changed and evolved over the past centuries. As in all of the Americas, there has been a fusion of ingredients, recipes, and cooking styles from across the world. Portugal, Native American, Angola, Nigeria, Spain, Italy, Germany, Japan, and most recently, China have all contributed to the food styles in different ways. However, enough remains of the traditional components and methods to form the basis of a unique regional cuisine. In addition, because of its strong base in local produce, many of the dishes and ingredients are not found beyond the Amazon region.

As a region renowned for its biodiversity, the multitude of fruits and vegetables available as the basis of this cuisine is enormous. Several of these "exotic" fruits, *guaraná* and *açaí* in particular, are becoming very well known throughout Brazil and abroad. *Guaraná* is the titular ingredient in an extremely popular soft drink found throughout Brazil and, more recently, throughout the world. Furthermore, it has become increasingly popular as a key ingredient in a number of energy drinks in the United States and Europe.[1] Fruits like *açaí* and *cupuaçu* have also garnered worldwide attention as "superfoods," high in health-giving properties (a phenomenon that will be discussed further in Chapter 4).

The main market in the city of Belém, Pará, near the mouth of the Amazon, is called the *Ver-o-Peso*.[2] It stretches along the riverfront and the small adjacent harbor. This market is really three or four separate markets, each specializing in a different type of produce. The market that opens earliest in the morning (at dawn or before) is the *açaí* market. The *açaí* vendors arrive by boat before first light and unload hundreds of wicker baskets of fruit (called *jamaxis*). The fruit is sold by the basket, not by the kilo: the price is approximately R$15 per *jamaxi*, and slightly more for the white variety of *açaí*. These vendors also sell coconuts, bananas, manioc, *farinha*, pigs, and other agricultural products from the rural regions along the Amazon and its tributaries. After they sell their wares, they shop on the quay near the *açaí* market for staples to take back to their homes upriver. Flour, vegetables, rice, and car batteries are all loaded back onto the boat along with the emptied *jamaxi* baskets for the next load of *açaí* to be brought to market. In the market clearing, the buyers of *açaí* transfer the berries into big plastic sacks and cart them off to the market, restaurants, stores, and delivery vans. Almost all the business transactions of this market are over by 7:30 in the morning.

The next area of the market to come to life is the fish market. The activity around the fish market dominates the harbor from early morning to midday. Here the fresh fish are unloaded from the fleet of fishing boats that dock each morning in the harbor, and are either sold directly on the dock by the fishermen themselves, or are transported across the street to the municipal fish market where fishmongers scale, cut, fillet, and otherwise prepare the fish for household and/or restaurant use. Fish come from the river, sea, and tributaries (the *river* here refers to the Amazon) in staggering diversity and plentitude. Many indigenous people derive a significant proportion of their diet from fish. These inland groups prefer freshwater fish to saltwater species. At the market, however, urban households and restaurants buy fish from all these environmental niches.

The fish markets are most robust in their early hours of operation. It is a scene of bustling shoppers, crying vendors, and clanking wheelbarrows. By noon the docks are hosed down and the indoor fish market is closing down as well. Relative quiet is achieved when the refrigerator trucks parked on the edge of the quay depart for markets to the south bearing their loads of fresh seafood.

The meat market across the street is also most lively in the early morning as shipments arrive and shopkeepers, market vendors from the satellite markets, and restaurateurs arrive. The smaller purchasers, housewives and *barraca* vendors, arrive later.

By contrast, the fruit and vegetable market of the *Ver-o-Peso* is open from sunrise to sunset and beyond. Here vendors group according to their wares—a section for fruits, one for nuts, another for vegetables, and others for smoked meat, dried shrimps, potions and perfumes, fruit pulp, grated manioc, *farinhas* (flours and

Figure 3.1 *Ver-o-Peso* Market in the salted fish section. Photograph by Jane Fajans.

meals), gourds and baskets, exotic plants, clothing, CDs, hammocks, and shoes. Alongside these stalls (*barracas*) are food stalls where one can purchase morning *mingaus* (porridge) of corn, *farinha*, tapioca, banana, or *açaí*. Later in the day, these *barracas* turn to lunch serving fried fish, soup, and regional specialties. They serve *salgados* (salted snacks) such as fried fish balls, chicken thighs, hot dogs, and *pasteis* (a deep fried dough pouch with either a sweet or savory filling) throughout the rest of the day and into the evening. These small stalls typically have a counter and five or six stools and a fairly regular clientele of market workers and other downtown employees. Here one can watch *açaí* being transformed from berry to soup or pudding, and eat the results of this process while looking at a row of T-Shirts proclaiming *açaí* as the heart of Pará. The last part of the market holds everything from DVDs to pots, batteries, hammocks, shoes, and T-shirts (Leitão 2010).

The *Ver-o-Peso* is one of the most famous markets in Brazil and an iconic image of Belém featured on numerous postcards, pamphlets, and tourist guides, not to mention being the subject of several poems and songs (de Lima 2010: 71). It is viewed as a cultural patrimony of the region and thus holds value beyond its role as a venue for food and goods. Residents of Belém refer to the market as one of the things to have pride in. Everyone I met in Brazil who had been to Belém waxed enthusiastic about the *Ver-o-Peso*. It is also one of the places migrants miss most.

As a venue for food and drinks, the market is a cornucopia of fruits, vegetables, herbs, flowers, land and sea animals, raw, processed, and cooked food. Although

Figure 3.2 A variety of different *farinhas* available in the *Ver-o-Peso* Market. Photograph by Jane Fajans.

many of the Amazonian ingredients are exported from the region as natural, healthful, and pure products, many are only available locally or have to be specially carried to other regions by migrants returning from the north or by specialty restaurant providers. While some of these ingredients can be eaten directly from the plants they grow on, others require a good deal of work in the form of production and preparation before they are fit for consumption.

This chapter is about eating in the Amazon region, especially in Belém, and about the foods and customs that are unique to this region. Most southern Brazilians do not know much about the food and diverse history of the Amazon. In fact, they often do not recognize that the region has a "history" since they associate the Amazon with a wild and untamed, and not a lived in, space. Those who acknowledge the long history and well-established set of traditions of the inhabitants of Amazonian states are usually those who have visited the area and have experienced at first hand the multitudinous foods and historical customs the region offers. Paraense food, in particular, contains textures, flavors, and sensations that are remarkably different from the rest of Brazilian food, and beyond. Either the foods do not travel well, or no one has thought it worth transporting them, so they are not widely found outside the region.[3]

Different methods of preparation can dramatically alter the tastes and textures of food. Chefs use this understanding of foods and techniques to create novel and desirable dishes. Such differences also create variations across regions and changes over time. As we saw in Chapter 2, several signature dishes span the region from Bahia to Pará but are subtly different in each place because of differences in preparation requiring the addition or subtraction of key ingredients.

Local Cuisine

In addition to their substantive and nourishing qualities, many of these foods have symbolic and medicinal properties. In part their symbolic associations come from their indigenous origins.

> But Amazonian cuisine is the most potent proof of the cultural superiority of the indigenous civilizations of the Amazon. For more than two hundred years, between 1530 and 1790, the Europeans were confronted by their own inferiority. To survive they had to adapt themselves to the native customs, cast off their velvet attire and heavy armor and rediscover the clothing of their first creation...
>
> The Belem table in 1665 was totally indigenous, a permanent feast of roast fish, game and seasonal fruits. (Bosisio 2000: 130)

In adapting to life in the Amazon, early colonists discovered daily life was eased by making use of the products and customs already adapted to the environment and readily accessible. Indigenous groups introduced the colonists to many of these foods. Many still retain the seminal nutritive, curative, and symbolic properties acquired in these encounters along with a version of a myth for each that elaborates the origin of these plants and how humans learned to use them. Although the region is replete with diverse indigenous peoples, in most cases the name of the food and the most pervasive stories of their origin are associated with the Tupi-speaking tribes first contacted by the colonists, who taught the explorers and settlers about these foods. The nutritive and folk medicinal uses of the foods that they taught the settlers remain the basis of their uses to this day. Recently, however, curious scientists from North America, Europe, and Brazil itself have begun to investigate the properties of many Amazonian food plants, such as *açaí*, *buriti*, *cupuaçu*, and *guaraná*, to discover the chemical basis for their storied nutritive and pharmacological properties. In the next chapter, I examine how some of these products have attracted a lot of recent attention in the media and foreign markets and how many of the local properties of the foods are becoming lost in translation from one community to another.

Making Many out of One: Manioc Six Ways

In some cases, a basic foodstuff can be transformed by indigenous methods into a variety of intermediate and final products with distinctly different tastes, textures, and qualities. Manioc is an exemplary foodstuff showcasing the many ways that a culture impresses its form and values on the production of food.

Manioc (*Manihot esculenta*) is one of the most important starchy staples in the world, although it is indigenous to Central and South America. Nowadays, it provides the main caloric component of much of the world's people in Africa, Latin America, and Southeast Asia. Manioc has been termed "the bread of Brazil" because of its ubiquitous manifestations in the traditional diet (EMBRAPA 2005). It is foundational to a great variety of foods and dishes in Brazil, and furthermore, can be used as a supplemental function in numerous other foods and dishes. Manioc/mandioca/cassava provides, beyond a doubt, one of the most varied and fascinating examples of how a food can be transformed by sophisticated cultural technologies into an amazing variety of useful forms. This process of transformation is certainly not unique to manioc; one can look at the multiple byproducts of corn, wheat, or soy as other examples. But manioc has been processed into at least six other products for centuries. I will examine these six uses of manioc in a discussion of *Paraense* food, but virtually all of this discussion holds true for Brazil's other Amazonian states.

Mandioca (the Portuguese term) is well known throughout Brazil and other parts of Latin America as the food from which *farinha* comes. But *farinha* is only one of five products of the manioc plant (and one additional and lesser known but significant variant) that anchors Amazonian and Brazilian gastronomy. The main foods derived from manioc are *farinha*, *tucupí*, *tapioca*, *maniva*, *goma*, and *tiquira*. Of these six foods, *farinha*, *tapioca*, and *goma* are widely known and used as staples in dishes and *bolos* (cakes) around the country. *Tucupí*, *tiquira*, and *maniva* are almost entirely restricted to use in the Amazonian regions and are difficult to find outside of them. I will detail several reasons why this might be so.

Manioc differs from many other widely consumed food plants because it possesses potentially poisonous properties. Manioc contains several compounds that can combine to form hydrocyanic acid.[4] These compounds are found in varying proportions in different plants depending on factors of *terroir* such as soil, age of plant, rainfall, and amount of nitrogen in the environment. Not all manioc tubers are poisonous, but without rigorous testing it is not obvious which plants may be toxic. Because of its poisonous properties, most manioc is processed to remove the juice that contains the toxins.[5] The Amerindian peoples who have cultivated this plant for millennia have developed a variety of processes to make it palatable. Preparation takes on added importance, and the work required to make it edible adds to the value people impart to the food. Manioc forms a basic staple in the Brazilian national and regional diets. Not all of the parts of the plant are used across the country, but some components enjoy near universal use while others are more narrowly and sparingly used. Different parts of the plant are processed by different techniques. The tuber can be grated, squeezed, sieved, baked, toasted, and boiled. The juice can be fermented, seasoned, and boiled; and the leaves can be cooked to the point of overdoneness.

For years common wisdom held that there were two kinds of manioc, which were assumed to be two different species: bitter and sweet. Nowadays, it is understood that all manioc is one species but the proportion of poison varies greatly depending on environmental factors (EMBRAPA 2005). In folk taxonomy, however, people still differentiate between *mandioca* (bitter manioc) and *aipim* or *macaxeira* (sweet manioc). Sweet manioc roots can be cooked and eaten rather like a yam or potato; they are often served boiled and puréed or fried like French fries. This sweet type of manioc is eaten in other parts of the world where the toxins are less prevalent in the soil so the tuber is less likely to be dangerous. It was grown and eaten like a tuber where I worked in Papua New Guinea.

Bitter manioc must be processed. Although manioc can be and often is poisonous, the key compound that makes it so, cyanic acid, is unstable and breaks down when heated. Once the tuber is well cooked it can be eaten safely; for this reason, one can understand how people were able to add manioc to their diet with only a little experimentation. However, even when prussic acid (another term for hydrocyanic acid) is no longer dangerous, it retains a bitter taste. To render the manioc less bitter, Amerindian cooks invented the process of removing the poisonous and bitter juices from the manioc tuber. They do this by scraping the tuber on a grater and making a pulp. The grated pieces are put in a *tipiti* (a woven cylindrical sieve that compresses when stretched) and squeezed until all the liquid runs out.[6] The poisonous liquid, however, is not discarded. Instead, it is further processed into several other components. Each of these components is an important part of the Amazonian diet. After drying, the grated pieces of manioc root are rubbed through a sieve to break them up. The resulting particles are then toasted to make *farinha*. *Farinha* is a dry, granular meal that can be eaten cold and dry, and can be stored for extended periods. It has become a staple of the Brazilian diet throughout virtually the entire country. As such, it is the most widely used product of the manioc plant.[7] Although the process of manufacturing it is now highly industrialized in the large manioc-growing regions of Central and Southern Brazil, the small-scale, artisanal form of *farinha* production is still prevalent in many parts of the Amazon region including indigenous and peasant communities. In indigenous communities, not all the grated manioc pieces are made into *farinha*, however, as we will see.

After separating the *farinha* from the liquid, the liquid is allowed to settle. During this phase, a fine starch or paste (*goma*) settles on the bottom of the dish while the liquid rises to the top and is then poured off. *Goma*, or manioc starch, used as a thickener or base for various dishes, is an important end product but can also be further processed into tapioca. Meanwhile, the poisonous juices are also further processed to become *tucupí*, which is used as a sauce or broth for local foods. After being separated from the rest of the manioc tuber, *tucupí* has to be left to stand for a few days. This liquid is then boiled and often seasoned with peppers and herbs. Many producers have their private seasoning recipes. *Tucupí* is an artisanal product, made in small batches by individual or family-run enterprises, and sold the same way. Once *tucupí* has been prepared, it is no longer poisonous; however, it does retain a slightly acid and astringent taste that can make the mouth slightly numb. Used as a sauce served on meats and fish, *tucupí* is also used as a basis for the soup *tacacá*. In addition, *tucupí* is used as a condiment and is frequently served in separate dishes on the table at meal-time. As a sauce, *tucupí* renders the meat so soft that "it melts in your mouth." *Tucupí* is often combined with an Amazonian leaf called *jambú* (*Acmella oleracea*), which, both raw and cooked, makes the mouth tingle as if it had just received a mild bolt of electricity. The combination of the acid numbness of *tucupí* and the tingly jolt of the *jambú* make these Amazonian dishes very distinct from other Brazilian cuisines.

Tucupí is primarily made in homes or small businesses. It is sold in recycled bottles in the market or in *barracas* (stalls) on the street. There is a section of the *Ver-o-Peso* dedicated to this product. It is not exported to other parts of the country, although it is sometimes hand carried to friends and relatives living outside the region who crave its unique taste. The process of making *tucupí* has a history closely related to the indigenous peoples of the Amazon who first prepared it, but today it is widely pre-pared and consumed by all the people of the region. It has become a key component in the regional cuisine. *Tucupí* is used in several dishes quintessential to Amazonian and Paraense cuisine. Primary dishes include *tacacá* (a soup made of *tucupí*, *goma*, *jambú*, and dried shrimp) and *pato no tucupí* (duck in *tucupí* sauce). These dishes ap-pear on most of the regional menus in Belém, and are offered in venues ranging from street corner stands to small stalls in the market; they are frequently served at family get-togethers, as well as being on menus in the fancier restaurants in town.

Despite their renown in the Amazon, *tacacá* and *pato no tucupí* are rarely found outside of the region, except in a few places in Bahia and in the Feira do Norte in São Cristoval in Rio. When they are found in such places in other parts of Brazil, they are primarily eaten by migrants from the Amazonian region (according to waiters at these restaurants). The ingredients for these foods are not found in stores in other parts of Brazil. They have to be brought by friends or relatives from the North, thus under-scoring the sense that these foods represent and are shared by a community. While *açaí* (see Chapter 4) is valued in Pará for its ability to "root" people to the place, dishes with *tucupí* instantiate the nostalgia that Paraense and other Amazonian resi-dents feel when they move away. These dishes are the first ones that returnees want when they come home and the ones they seek to re-create when afar (Martins 2009).

One can find stands, carts, and street corner vendors selling *tacacá* most after-noons in Belém. A late afternoon snack of this tingly soup has become a custom in this tropical city. The habit of taking a gourdful of *tacacá* is not just a food event, but something of a social event as well. Many of the *tacacá* vendors have a steady and devoted clientele who patronize the same stand for years. They develop social rela-tions with the vendor, often in a mother-son type of relationship that contains a value of nurture and familiarity (Rural 2009; de Roberts and van Velthem 2009).

Tacacá

Ingredients

1 lb. of manioc starch (*goma*)

1 liter of *tucupí*

1½ lbs. of dried shrimp (or prawns)

3 bunches of *jambú*

3 *pimentas de cheiro* (hot yellow peppers from the Amazon)

1 tb. of salt

2 tbs. of crushed garlic

1 bunch of chicory

1 bunch of basil

Preparation

1. Shell the shrimps, leaving the tails, and let soak for 2 hours changing the water two or three times.
2. Boil the *tucupí* for 40 minutes with a little salt, chicory, basil, and garlic.
3. Clean the *jambú*, leaving the stems; wash well and boil for 30 minutes.
4. Boil three liters of water with the rest of the salt and gradually add the manioc starch, stirring well to prevent it from going lumpy.
5. Allow to cook for 30 minutes until it is a thick gruel.
6. Crush the *pimenta de cheiro* with 4 tablespoons of *tucupí*.
7. Serve in black gourds, putting a little *tucupí*, a ladle of gruel, several *jambú* leaves, and four prawns.
8. Mix the *tucupí* with the gruel. (Bosisio 2000: 143)

Figure 3.3 *Tacacá* served in a traditional gourd bowl. Photograph by Jane Fajans.

The *tacacaeiro/a* (*tacacá* vendor) serves the soup in a traditional fashion, in a gourd bowl called a *cuia*, often with incised designs on it. The gourd may be seated in a wicker basket that holds it upright or held directly in both hands while sipped. A toothpick is provided to lift the shrimp or *jambú* leaves to the mouth, otherwise the soup is drunk directly from the bowl. Most locals acknowledge that this dish is of indigenous origin. Certainly the ingredients are local and have been used for years (Bosisio 2002: 131; Camara Cascudo 1983: vol. 1). In addition to its popularity as an afternoon snack, the dish is an important component of the big religious festival, the *Cirío*, which celebrates the Virgin of Nazarré and is held in Belém on the second Sunday in October.

One of the many charming T-shirts sold at the open air markets around Belém is entitled "*Ser Paraense é...*," which translates as "To be Paraense is..." It has a list of thirty-three qualities that define the true Paraense (resident of Pará), of which fourteen involve food.[8] This ranges from "eating *açaí* either with or without sugar" to eating "almost everything with *farinha*."[9] An important one says that to be a Paraense "one must drink a gourdful of *tacacá* during the hottest time at three in the afternoon." This T-shirt elicited loving commentary from my two Paraense companions who stroked each line of the shirt and elaborated on how each fit with their own experience as "Paraenses."

Another aspect of popular culture extolling *tacacá* is featured in a popular song in Pará called "*Garota do Tacacá*," or the "*Tacacá* Girl," which describes some of the processes that go into making the soup and the relationship with the *tacacaeira*. A friend in upstate New York sang me this song as we reminisced about Paraense food and she experienced nostalgia for the tastes and smells of her home. Later she sent me links to several performances of this song on YouTube (Pinduca 2009).

Garota do Tacacá

Oi mexe mexe menina,
Vamos mexer sem parar,
Você agora é a minha garota do tacacá—
Rala rala mandioca,
Espreme no tipiti,
Separa a tapioca,
Apara o *tucupí*,
Prepara o meu tacacá,
Gostoso como açai.[10]

(Ferreira 2010)

The *Feira de Norte* in Rio de Janeiro is a large, covered fairground containing northeastern Brazilian food, books, and crafts; it is also a venue for *Nordestino* music and dance events.[11] It serves as a gathering place for many of the migrants who have moved south to escape the poverty and unemployment of the Northeast. Among the dozens of restaurants oriented to the *Nordestinos*, there is a single restaurant offering Amazonia specialties such as *tacacá, pato no tucupí,* and *açaí.* According to the restaurant staff, the principal clients at this restaurant are Paraense migrants who are homesick for these foods. The ingredients such as *tucupí, jambú,* and *açaí* all have to be imported from the Amazonian region.

A second signature dish of the Amazon region is *pato no tucupí,* duck with *tucupí* sauce. Although *tucupí* works as a sauce in which numerous species of fish and kinds of meats can be cooked, it particularly enhances fatty meats and fish such as duck and *pirarucu* (an Amazonian fish). The sauce seems to draw the grease out of the meat and render it very tender. The *tucupí* gives the dish a slightly astringent taste since the sauce has numbing properties. This dish is a festive one, served for special family occasions. According to Paulo Martins, chef and owner of the restaurant *Lá en Casa,* it is the dish that evokes the most nostalgia from Paraenses, especially those living away from the region (Martins 2007).

In addition to *farinha, goma,* and *tucupí,* the manioc plant is processed into several other foods, *tapioca, puba, maniva,* and *tiquira. Tapioca* is widely known both inside and outside Brazil. *Tapioca* is made from the fine paste or starchy flour that washes off the manioc flour. This fine paste is passed through a special sieve that creates uniform lumps or balls. These balls are roasted at a low temperature and the lumps burst open, creating *tapioca* pearls, a translucent and somewhat gelatinous ball of starch used for soups, porridges, drinks, and desserts. *Tapioca* is frequently eaten as a porridge,[12] often flavored with banana or *açaí.* One of the principal forms of *tapioca* is *beiju,* a pancake or crepe made of *tapioca,* and served dry, hot with butter or coconut milk or folded over a filling like a rice cake.[13] In parts of the Northeast of Brazil, and increasingly in other regions around the country, *tapiocarias* (*tapioca* stands) are a very popular form of fast food stall. These stalls provide fast food along the beaches, at festival gatherings, and are even opening as restaurants. Here the *tapioca* is poured into a thin pancake-like circle on a griddle and the resulting crepes are served folded over both sweet and savory fillings.

Another important product from the manioc root is *carimã* or *puba* (meaning "rotten" in Tupi, an indigenous language) (Fernandes 2000). *Carimã* is essentially fermented manioc that can be made into a flour or meal. The shredded manioc pulp is soaked in water and becomes mildly fermented. If left moist, the dough is called *puba,* and can be made into fine flour by pushing it through a sieve. If this pulp is dried, it is called *carimã* and often forms granules called *farinha de água.* People who have grown up eating this kind of *farinha* rather than the standard *farinha* miss its sourdough-like taste. Friends living in places like Brasilia described having to have friends and relatives send them a steady supply from the north. One person described how his family went through 10 kilos of *farinha de água* a month because his wife and children adored it. He implied, but did not say, that he was not as avid a consumer, having grown up in the south rather than the north of the country. *Carimã* can be used as a base for porridges (*mingau*), couscous, and cakes. Finer granules of *puba* are made into flour used in bread and cakes.

Most of the foods described thus far are made from the tubers of the manioc plant. *Maniva* is the exception. It is made from the leaves of the plant. These leaves are also potentially toxic. To overcome this problem, the method of preparation requires prolonged cooking. Informant accounts of how long they cooked the leaves varied from three to fifteen days. Cookbooks usually specify seven days, but each cook has his or her own opinion about this. The leaves are picked before the plant is fully mature. Mature leaves contain more toxins. They are then finely shredded (often this is done by distributors in the market, not at home). The leaves may be sold shredded and raw or may be sold cooked, allowing the customer to take home the leaves and immediately add them to the dish *maniçoba*, the primary dish that uses *maniva* leaves as a bean substitute. *Maniçoba* is a stew composed of most of the same ingredients as *feijoada* (see Chapter 6), which is a big bean stew with pork (including the ear, tail, feet, and tongue), dried beef, *lingüiça*, and smoked meats. Instead of the black or brown beans commonly found in *feijoada*, *maniçoba* uses *maniva* leaves. This creates a thick, dense stew that has a very earthy taste. It is served with rice, *farinha de água*, and *pimenta de cheiro*.[14] This dish is hardly ever found outside of the Amazon region, nor is it well known elsewhere, although it is just beginning to be found in some restaurants in the South. The enormous time and effort involved in producing this dish, however, gives it a unique place in the local cuisine, and these same qualities have kept it embedded in that locality. In Pará a local cook can buy many of the ingredients semiprepared in the market. The *maniva* leaves can be purchased precooked and the selection of meats is sold in combination packages at market stalls specializing in smoked and dried meats. This combination of meats is very similar to those used in *feijoada* and the dish is often seen to fill the same slot as *feijoada*, being served for extended family meals on Saturday. The thick stew of mushy leaves and well-cooked meats, which have given their flavor to the leaves and liquid, has a heavy and somewhat distinct taste. Those unaccustomed to the taste may describe it as "earthiness or muddiness," but others say that the taste grows on one quickly. Restaurant cooks and waiters say that most of the local/regional dishes are ordered and eaten by local residents. Foreigners tend to try one or two but do not like them and then stick to more familiar fare. Everyone said it was hard to prepare this food outside of the region because the ingredients need to be fresh and do not transport well.

A final way that manioc enters the diet is in the age-old form of alcohol. A drink called *Tiquira* is a specialty of Maranhão, the state neighboring Pará to the east. Here they make a violet/deep pink liquor from grated manioc root. The tuber is peeled, grated, and pressed to remove the juice, following the steps used to make *farinha*. The resulting pulp is then toasted on a hot griddle, as if one were making *farinha* or *beijus*. The resulting pancake is then left in the open air to absorb the various yeasts from the environment. In three or four days the dough turns pink with the fungus and yeast. This microbe-covered *beiju* is then crumbled into a large trough of a hollowed log (at least that's how it was done traditionally) and covered with water. It is mixed daily and in about forty-eight hours has finished its fermentation. The liquid is then distilled in an *alembique* (a copper still) and the resulting alcohol is bottled (Maranhão 2010). The alcohol content of this product is between 34 to 58 percent. This particular version of a manioc-based alcoholic beverage is not well known except in the Amazon region of Maranhão, but indigenous versions of fermented manioc drinks made in a wood trough (but not distilled) appear in the ethnographies on several Amazonian tribes. Some of these methods of making "manioc beer" among such Amerindian groups include a preliminary step in which women, usually designated as "old women," chew and then spit the pulp into the trough. Their enzyme-laden saliva serves to initiate the fermentation process. The *chicha* or beer produced in this way in indigenous villages is frequently much less alcoholic, ranging from 3 to 6 percent (Turner 2011).

For many years, the basic flour in Brazil was manioc flour, which gives substance to the saying, "Manioc, the bread of Brazil." Manioc flour was the default flour that could be bought relatively cheaply in the store. Wheat flour, *farinha de trigo*, was the marked and less common type of flour that was reserved for special occasions. Only recently has the production and importation of wheat made this type of flour more common than the native type (Lopes 2009). With the arrival of many newer European immigrants at the end of the nineteenth century and beginning of the twentieth, the desire for "real" flour increased and it became more common. Interestingly, nowadays, with the rise of gluten intolerance, products made with manioc flour (gluten-free flour) are experiencing a resurgence.

As we can see, the importance of manioc as a staple food transcends the simple daily act of consuming it. Manioc has become a basic food in many forms with multiple uses. Each form is in a way more complex than the last. Of course, not all foods can be treated in this richly symbolic way, but it is amazing to find one food that takes such different forms and fills so many niches. It is no wonder that cassava has become such a staple of the South American (and now world) diet. It is only in Pará and contiguous parts of other Amazonian states, however, that all six of the original methods for processing manioc and their distinctive food products remain vital parts of the regional culture. Manioc in its many forms contributes, perhaps more fundamentally than any other factor, to the distinctive Amazonian cultural identity of Pará.

To an outsider, the various end products of manioc processing are so different as not to appear part of a continuous unitary process at all, but to those who enact the processes of manioc production or other highly transformative processes, the different principles of gastronomic transformation become readily and frequently evident. In a number of Amazonian societies, the process of food production symbolically reflects the process of life and social transformation (C. Hugh-Jones 1978). Putting a meal together symbolically encompasses the activities of men and women, of natural and social processes, and the labor that underlies these components. What you eat, therefore, symbolizes more than the need all living things have for nutrition, as important as that is, nor are the socially defined values of who eats what and with whom the only considerations.

Many of these forms of manioc have become so embedded in the national diet that they no longer convey any properties of their social origin or ecological context. They have lost this indigenous heritage and even their Amazonian origin. In common with the Paraense habit of putting *farinha* on everything, many southern Brazilians do the same; it is often found in bowls on both restaurant and family tables and used as a garnish on everything. In addition, large numbers of Brazilians eat *pão de queijo*, a small cheese roll made out of manioc starch and Mineiran cheese, which has become a breakfast staple and snack across the country and one of the most beloved of Brazilian exports. Fried *aipim* or *macaxeira* (sweet manioc) takes the place of French fries on many menus. These forms of manioc are found across the nation but are recognized not as an indigenous or Amazonian food, but as a marker of Brazilianness. In sum, although many people both within and beyond the Amazon now consume numerous Amazonian products, the regional associations for many of these edibles have been lost, and they have taken on a generic Brazilian identity. Those ingredients and recipes that retain a specific regional and indigenous identity are those that have not found wide acceptance outside the region, either because they do not travel well or because they appear very different to southern Brazilian palates as kinds of comestibles.

Other Amazonian Foods

Manioc is not the only staple inherited from the indigenous peoples of the Americas. Corn, peppers, and many varieties of beans remain key ingredients in both the indigenous diet and that of the national cuisine. In particular, corn plays a significant role in Brazilian culture. Several aspects of its symbolic importance were discussed in Chapter 2, but here I briefly consider corn's centrality in its Amerindian context. Although not as prominent in the daily diet, cornmeal, *fuba*, is important in porridges, cakes, and other dishes. Steamed, roasted, or boiled corn on the cob is a frequent snack available at the beach or in the town plazas from carts and stalls. Cornmeal, *masa*, is prepared by wrapping it in corn husks like tamales and steaming it. The filling of this dish, *pamonha*, can be sweet or savory. Green corn ice cream is also a popular flavor, which despite our association with corn, is a sweet flavor.

Corn is also symbolically important for many of the indigenous tribes of the Amazon. Many of these groups share a ritual called the New Corn Ceremony. The myth that accompanies this ceremony in some Gê tribes like the Kayapó of Pará describes how the different Amazonian tribes came to diverge (Turner 2011). The myth begins when the corn plant was still a giant tree from which all people ate. The people decided to chop down the tree to harvest the kernels that grow on its branches in order to create multiple transplants and increase the quantity of corn produced and their access to that production. When they did this, groups formed to plant the kernels in different places. This dispersal created not only physical but linguistic distance: they immediately began speaking different languages. Unable to communicate with the other groups, whose languages were mutually incomprehensible, the groups scattered across the landscape and formed different tribes (Turner 2011).

Festive Foods

Corn is especially important in June, during the June Festivals mentioned earlier in the book, especially in the Central West, North, and Northeast of Brazil (see Chapter 2). In the Amazon, the *Festas Juninas* are in many ways more important and popular than *Carnaval*, which is usually promoted as the biggest celebration in Brazil (Pace 2009). Many friends and acquaintances told me that if I were interested in food I had to come back for the *Festas Juninas* because special food was part of the ritual and these foods were predominantly corn-based. Some had me believe that corn and only corn was the core of the festival. So, I have made it a point to return to Brazil several times for the June Festivals. My first year, attending the festival in Cruz das Almas, in Bahia, I searched high and low for corn dishes and was sorely disappointed to find none. In later years, I did find a number of these dishes exactly as my friends had described, but I also found these dishes intermixed with other snack foods or served on other occasions in numerous places.

The Amazon as Indigenous

Amazonian food and culture retain a strong connection to the indigenous populations who inhabited the region in precolonial times and who continue to hunt, fish, and farm gardens on territorial reserves over which they have been steadily gaining rights. Even though the majority of people now identifying as Amazonian or Paraense are not of indigenous descent, or do not recognize such descent, many of them live in ways that are compatible with the indigenous lifestyle. Many rural residents and dwellers along the great rivers farm, hunt, and gather in ways reminiscent of indigenous cultures, and learned much of their techniques for planting their *roças* (small garden plots) with manioc, corn, rice, and beans from the indigenous peoples around them (Acevedo and de Castro 2004; Carneiro da Cunha and Almeida 2000). They also use the Amazon forest to supplement their livelihoods and earn cash by extracting rubber, Brazil nuts, and *açaí*. In these ways, the immemorial culture of the Amazon and the perpetuation of it as a lived environment remains an important, continuous aspect of regional identity. Many of these groups perform the same activities as the indigenous people around them, but may have very different views on the meaning and value of these activities.

The Kayapó

Among a number of indigenous groups of the Amazon, basic foods tend to be associated with genders. The realms in which these foods are procured are also gendered. At the most basic level, these associations are based on associations through the division of labor. Tasks that men do are symbolically male, as are the fruits of their labor; tasks that women do are seen as female and so are the things they produce. Among the Kayapó of Southern Pará and Northern Mato Grosso, men are the principal hunters and fishers. The various meats they garner are coded as symbolically male when they appear in a meal. Women are responsible for the majority of horticultural produce and these foodstuffs are symbolically female. In their gardens they grow manioc, corn, squash, banana, plantains, tobacco, a vine-like green called *kupa*, and nowadays black beans, fava beans, and dry rice. Around the villages they plant avocado trees. The ideal meal is a conjunction of male and female elements and is analogous to the ideal marriage (Turner 2012).

A similar idea emerges in C. Hugh-Jones's description of the Barasana of the Northwestern Amazon region. Again men provide meat or fish, which are valued as masculine components in the meal. Women provide the products from the garden: manioc, maize, squash. In addition to these two basic categories, the Barasana have a third important element to their meal. The women make a spicy condiment that is served with the meat and starches. This condiment is made from hot peppers rendered into a thick sauce. The pepper sauce adds spice to the meal and represents the spice of sexuality (particularly female sexuality) in a marriage. It is the component that unites the genders (C. Hugh-Jones 1978).

A frequent meal for the Kayapó is a "meat pie" in which pieces of meat are embedded in a manioc dough and cooked in an earth oven. The earth oven, *ki*, is a woman's responsibility. In front or to the side of her house, she builds a fire to heat large stones, and when they are hot, covers them with leaves. She places the meat pie on the stones and covers it with more leaves and hot stones, and then tops the whole assemblage with earth to hold the heat and moisture in. The food essentially steams in the oven. The house and oven are a unit and are called *ki kre* ("the space of the oven") and represent the social living space of the family (Turner 2012). The meat pie is an amalgam of the male and female tasks in which each component remains discrete but each flavors and adds to the other.

Among the Kayapó the day-to-day division of labor and the unification of the genders in the construction of a meal becomes magnified in the preparations and consumption of the communal feast that accompanies the climax of the performance of every major ceremony. The normal pattern of hunting is exponentially increased as groups of men spend extended periods of time searching for meat to feast on during the ceremony. They search for tortoises in particular since these animals can be kept alive with little effort until needed for the ritual. They continually smoke the meats that cannot be kept alive to preserve them. While the men are trekking to hunt for meat, the women work to amass large quantities of manioc from their gardens and bring them to the village. There they process them into *puba* (manioc flour) and sourdough-like *masa*. Women also collect large stones and lumps of dry earth to heat for the earth oven.

The feasts during the communal ceremonies are like the family meals writ large. Instead of individuals providing components of the meals, groups of men and groups of women provide for the entire village. The earth ovens are much larger than those used in everyday cooking, and the meat pies are enormous. The members of the community are creating their community by collectively working and consuming the products that symbolize their identities. The principal ceremonies with their feasts, in short, are sacred performances that reconstitute society while simultaneously enacting the making of social identity of girls as well as boys.

Kayapó men love to hunt and both men and women love to gorge on meat. A number of other Amazonian societies, however, are more reluctant meat-eaters (S. Hugh-Jones 1996). Many Amazonian peoples may only eat animals like *paca*, which are large rodents and not particularly aggressive. Attitudes toward meat are to a great degree correlated with modes of warfare or violence. The Kayapó often kill animals directly with clubs, rather than at a distance with bows and arrows. They find the chase and kill very exhilarating and do it as a collective activity. Club warfare is also their preferred mode of confronting an enemy. Groups upstream from them, the Upper Xinguano tribes, prefer to use bows and arrows for both warfare and hunting, and eat considerably less meat. They view the Kayapó practices as quintessentially barbaric. They see restraint in eating meat as a properly cultured attitude (S. Hugh-Jones 1996).

Amazonian Identity in a Changing Landscape

Amazonian food is deeply embedded in the indigenous past, but it has evolved and taken on multiple new aspects of identity as has the Amazon region itself. On the one hand, the Amazon has always had a place in the Brazilian imagination as a vast frontier that was ripe for development. Many have viewed it as a region of enormous unexploited resources of timber, gold, and energy, while offering huge tracts of land brimming with potential for cattle pasture or soy agriculture, laced with rivers teeming with fish and hydroelectric potential. On the other hand, the Amazon remains the largest natural forest in the world and contains the largest storehouse of carbon on the earth's surface. These features, combined with its incredible diversity in flora and fauna, make it very susceptible to overdevelopment and ecological devastation. Many residents in the region, including but not limited to the many indigenous peoples, are desperately concerned to protect the region for both themselves and the world at large (Turner 1999). A large coalition of international organizations has taken on the protection of the Amazon as their cause. Aligned against these local and international interests are very powerful forces including big industries, foreign investors, and powerful landowners. The conflicting perspectives of these many actors play a large role on the national stage. The combined result is that the Amazon and the traditional cultures of the region are in flux and at risk.

Because of international interest in the Amazon, national perceptions have changed in often unanticipated ways. Who owns the Amazon is contested. Social and environmental activists, both internal and external to Brazil, lobby intensely to protect the largest forest in the world from uncontrolled destruction, sometimes claiming this region as belonging to the global community and essential to the future of humanity. These advocates confront fervid nationalist claims that the forest belongs to Brazil for Brazil's exclusive use (at least the portions within Brazil's national borders). Both groups are often in competition with more localized regional and state claims, as well as those voiced by indigenous and nonindigenous residents alike. Few of these perspectives take into consideration the social and cultural aspects of the Amazon as a lived environment and home to millions of people. The meanings and values that *terroir*, foods, dishes, and commensality have in situ is a valuable part of culture. It is also very vulnerable. In the next chapter we will look at how certain foods significantly change their qualities, meanings, and values as they move away from the locus of customary practices into new environments and cultures.

–4–

Açaí: From the
Amazon to the World

In the public imagination, the Amazon epitomizes pure, unadulterated nature. Most of what we hear about the Amazon in the Western media focuses on its vast natural resources, its "raw" nature. Seen as healthy, generative, and potent, it has been called "the lungs of the earth"; its vast sea of trees renews much of the oxygen in the planet's atmosphere. People travel to the Amazon to see undisturbed environments and an abundance of biodiversity. Tourism focuses on plants and animals, natural phenomena, and "green" perspectives. Human activity is condoned if it is sustainable and nonintrusive, but human culture and communities are not the focus of tourism or protectionism (Carneiro da Cunha and Almeida 2000; Acevedo and Ramos de Castro 2000). In contrast to other parts of the country where people visit to experience history and culture and to enjoy leisure activities, those who visit the Amazonian region expect to see pure, uninhabited nature.

These general beliefs contrast with the representation of the Amazon as a lived environment laid out in Chapter 3. That description represented the Amazon as a region with a lived history, a variety of cultures and a deep sense of human involvement. In that chapter, the Amazon's environmental richness was fully acknowledged as offering tremendous possibilities for human engagement and exploitation. The Amazon was presented, at least in part, as a human environment in which different groups of people, from the indigenous communities to the small farmers and extractivists,[1] forged a living within the forest and riverine ecosystem. Beyond these small-scale inhabitants, large ranchers, miners, loggers, and soy farmers transform the ecology of areas that were once natural forest and savannah. The small farmers are almost invisible to the foreign eye, while the big developers have aroused worldwide antagonism for their exploitation leading to environmental devastation.

Caught between these discordant views of the symbolic importance of the Amazon are the interests of scientists and health food suppliers. The abundant flora and fauna hold potential value for markets beyond the region. These offerings range from plants with reputed medicinal potential, to fruits and vegetables with nutritive and folkloric curative properties.

Several of these "exotic" fruits, *guaraná*, *cupuaçu* (*Theobroma grandiflorum*), *bacuri* (*Platonia insignis*) and *açaí* in particular, are becoming very well known throughout Brazil and abroad. They are consumed by both local people, Brazilians outside of the region, and overseas aficionados. *Guaraná (Paullinia cupana)* forms the base of an extremely popular soft drink of the same name, found throughout Brazil and more recently throughout the world. In addition, the fruit has recently become a key ingredient in a number of energy drinks in the United States and Europe. *Açaí (Euterpe oleracea)* is a small, dark purple fruit from the Amazon. In Amazonia in general, and Pará in particular, it is a basic food, served as a juice, a soup-like porridge, a sauce, or a sweet dessert.[2] *Açaí* has also been used for a number of other purposes. Historically, Brazilians have used *açaí* berries to treat such disorders as digestive problems and skin conditions. Primarily valued as a food ingredient in Pará, it is the health-giving and medicinal properties of *açaí* that have become best known outside of the local region.

According to an indigenous myth, *açaí* is a plant that sprang up from the grave of a young baby, the granddaughter of a great chief. This chief tried to save his tribe from starvation by sacrificing all newborn children so as to keep the population from increasing. The first child thus killed was his own grandchild, causing great mourning and remorse on the part of his daughter, the baby's mother. She died of sorrow at the foot of the tree that grew from her baby's grave. This tree, the *açaí* palm, bore branches of small black fruits that enabled the chief to feed his people for years to come, and in so doing, prevented the need to commit further infanticide (Anon. 2012b). *Guaraná*, according to the Maué myth, comes from the eyes of a young man whose handsomeness, bravery, and generosity provoked the jealousy of a god who killed him out of spite. The fruit of this plant resembles the human eye from which it grew (Anon. 2009).

As we saw in the previous chapter, the various products of the Amazon are locally used as food and drink. The markets, restaurants, and homes in which these products are consumed are part of the social and historical landscape. The fact that lots of people have used these foods for centuries, if not longer, gives them value in the production of daily life, and salience in the hearts and minds of the inhabitants of Amazonian states.

Symbolic and medicinal properties augment the substantive and nourishing qualities of these foods. The symbolic associations come in part from their indigenous origins. From the earliest contact with Europeans, indigenous tribes have been feeding and healing those who have arrived on their shores. Local foods, as we have seen, played an important role in sustaining the earliest explorers. Local herbs and medicines did the same.

Although the region is replete with diverse indigenous tribes, in most cases, the name of the foods and the most pervasive stories of their origin derived from the Tupi-speaking tribes first contacted by the colonists who taught the explorers and settlers about these foods. The nutritive and medicinal uses with which these foods were associated have persisted.

Even today, the sections of the markets devoted to potions and perfumes made from native plants are centrally located and colorfully arrayed. Here one can find cures for arthritis, indigestion, headaches, constipation, colds, and impotence. In addition there are potions for love, sex, beauty, business, and monetary success. Other concoctions evoke mythic beliefs about pink river dolphins (*botos*) who turn into seducers. Still others protect people from strange demons who inhabit the deep woods. While all these are traditional remedies, the sections devoted to them in the markets capitalize on the fascination they hold for tourists, seemingly orienting themselves more to foreign trade than local clientele. Vivacious *barraqueiras*, market women, accost pedestrians (especially those with cameras) as they enter the perfume and medicine spaces of the market shouting cures for the ills they hastily diagnose in the passersby: how to attract a lover; how to achieve luck on a deal; and the most famous offering, and the one guaranteed to cause laughter, is the offer (to men) of *Viagra natural*, a concoction touted as curing impotence, and pushed on any male over the age of forty who enters their space.[3]

Recently, however, so-called Western science, in the form of both academic and private business research studies, has taken a look at the properties of many Amazonian plants, such as *açaí*, *buriti* (*Mauritia flexuosa*), *cupuaçu*, and *guaraná*, to discover their nutritive and pharmacological properties. I have chosen to discuss some of these products because they have attracted a lot of recent attention in the media and market but also because they have such a vital role in the daily life of Paraenses (*Açaí* 2011a,c; Colapinto 2011).

Figure 4.1 *Açaí* vendor selling *açaí* in the traditional *jamaxis* baskets at the *Açaí* Market in Belém. Photograph by Jane Fajans.

Açaí has a special place in the cuisine and identity of the people of Pará, especially those around the city of Belém. In Belém, there are several different *açaí* markets, scattered around town. Most of these satellite markets obtain their supply from the early morning market described in Chapter 3. Here, the vendors from smaller neighborhood markets purchase the fruit and transfer it into big plastic sacks, which they cart off to the neighborhood markets, while other buyers transport their purchases to restaurants, stores, and market stalls in delivery vans and wheelbarrows. Markets, restaurants, and even homes display the availability of *açaí* for sale by hanging a red banner, sign, or flag outside the door (Trevisani 2002). In this way, the availability of *açaí* appears as a public symbol for local food and hospitality. This notice differs from an ordinary commercial sign because it is only displayed when *açaí* is on offer, and serves as an invitation to enter and partake.

In addition to this folksy display of the local importance of *açaí*, its public value is promoted by the fact that the State of Pará has trademarked the logo *açaí*, in red lettering on a black background, as a symbol of the state. This logo is marketed on shirts, towels, bags, and hats. It has recently been elaborated and can be found in various colors and backgrounds on the same sorts of items. The fame of *açaí* contrasts with other important foods in Pará and the Amazon that are widely used in the cuisine but not iconized the same way. Why is this one food more famous and valued than other foods from this region? Why has it become a brand?

Regional Food

Açaí is a small palm fruit that grows in bunches on long stems from the top of the *açaí* palm. The fruits are stripped off the ropey stem and soaked in water. The softened fruit is then rubbed through a fine sieve, or nowadays an electric grater, to remove the thin layer of pulp from the seed within. The pulp of the fruit is added to water to make a violet-colored sauce or juice and is served in a variety of forms. A bowl of *açaí* may be consumed plain, but is usually combined with *tapioca* or *farinha* (toasted manioc meal), in which case it becomes a kind of porridge, *mingau*. *Açaí* dishes can be consumed with or without sugar (sweet or savory) as the line on the T-shirt discussed in the last chapter describes: "to be Paraense ... is to eat *açaí* with or without sugar." One common use of *açaí* in Paraense households is as an accompaniment for fish and meat, eaten alongside or used as a dipping sauce. In this sense, the traditional use of *açaí* differs from the uses most southern Brazilians, Europeans, or North Americans have come to expect. Locally it is most frequently served as a *salgado* or savory dish rather than just as a sweet porridge, smoothie, or dessert as it has come to be known elsewhere. As a sauce to accompany meat and grilled or fried fish, it is often used for dipping. As a dessert, it can be sweetened like a fruit soup or chilled and served as ice cream or popsicle flavoring; it can also be used in tarts, custards, and cakes (Facciola 1990 cited in Davidson 1999; Martins 2005).

Figure 4.2   The traditional serving of *açaí* with *tapioca* or *farinha*. Photograph by Jane Fajans.

Açaí is such an important part of life in the Amazon that it is served daily in many households. People often say "Without *açaí* I feel hungry" even if they have eaten a number of other foods (Sigueira 2010). In this sense Sigueira (2010) calls it a "validator" food, that is, a food ingredient that is so central to the composition of a meal that its presence defines a meal (Weismantel 1988: 125). As a staple food, *açaí* has been a relatively cheap source of calories and nutrition and thus, in Brazil, functions as a food of the poor.

Despite this traditional importance, *açaí* has become harder to find and more expensive to buy locally. There are multiple reasons for this, but the most significant is that much of the production is being siphoned off for export. Fresh *açaí* used to be grown by small producers who consumed it at home and brought the surplus to market and sold it in town. As demand and prices have risen, much of the produce is shipped directly to processing plants where it is pulped and frozen or freeze dried. Even small producers find it more profitable to sell their crop than to consume or market it in town. Only a small portion of the crop is still available to the populace at large, and consumers complain they are getting the poorer-quality fruits at a higher price (Colapinto 2011; Sigueira 2010; Brondízio 2008).

The poorer quality is a result of vastly increased production. Traditional *açaí* trees were planted on the river's edges and grew in this marshy environment. To meet increased demand, large plantations of *açaí* trees are being planted on newly cleared forest land often quite distant from the river's edge. Locals believe these new production practices result in inferior fruits. In addition, the sustainability of production has altered. What was once a small-scale activity that blended into the surrounding ecology has come to replace large tracts of the native forest. Although *açaí* is a native product, industrial production is much less sustainable for both plants and wildlife.

A further consequence of these changing production patterns is that the purple *açaí* has become far more common than the preferred white kind. The white variety is only known in the Amazon region, it is not used for the drinks or beverages that are exported from this region, so production of white *açaí* has been displaced by purple *açaí* production and it has become relatively scarcer and harder to find. Although most informants state that there is very little difference in taste between the two kinds, many locals prefer the white variety and are willing to pay a bit more to procure it when available. To know about white *açaí* is to claim one's identity as a local. To consume it, in lieu of the cheaper purple kind, is a mark of status.

An important aspect of these agricultural practices comes from the fact that in the eyes of most consumers of *açaí* outside of the Amazon, it embodies natural qualities of the "rainforest." The fact that it is planted and produced industrially is both unrecognized and to a large degree contradictory to the beliefs and values it conveys outside the region. These mixed conceptions about the origin and production of many if not most of the foods that we find in our grocery stores is a product of globalization. Many in the First World live with such contradictions all the time. Because *açaí* exemplifies so many symbolic properties of health, nature, and indigenous values, much of the marketing of this product portrays it as emanating from a pure and natural environment.

In Pará and the rest of the Amazon, *açaí* can appear in all parts of the meal. It can be part of *café da manhã* (breakfast) as a *mingau* or purée served with *farinha* or *tapioca*; it can be a dipping sauce for fish or *macaxeira* (sweet manioc); or it can be a flavoring used in cakes (*bolos*) or ice cream. In general, the verb to drink, *tomar*, is used in reference to *açaí*, indicating how the locals principally consume it.

A local song describes the importance of *açaí* and the local beliefs about it. It also describes the various ways of preparing and eating *açaí*:

> *Eu foi de vou plantar*
> *E pra que tu foi plantada*
> *Pra invadir a nossa mesa*
> *Pra abastar a nossa casa*
> *Teu distino foi traçado*
> *Pelas mãos de Mãe-do-mato*
> *Aos cuidados de uma deusa*
> *Cujo toque é bem suave*
> *Es a planta que dementa*
> *A paixão de nossa povo*
> *Macho-fêmea das touceiras*
> *Onde Oxossi faz seu posto*

A mais magra das palmeiras
Mas mulher do sangue grosso
É homen do angue vasto
Tu te entrega até o caroço
E tua fruta vai rolando
Para os nossos aiguaideres
Tu te entrega ao sacrifice
Fruta santa, fruta mârtir
Tens o dom de seres muito
Onde muitos não tem nada
Uns te chaman açaizeiro
Outros te chaman juçara
Põe tapioca
Põe farinha d'água
Põe açucar
Não põe nada
Ou me bebe como suco
Eu so muito mais que um fruto
Sou saber marajoara
Sou sabor marajoara.[4]

As this song shows, the *açaí* tree is treated with reverence and associated with the Afro-Brazilian deity *Oxossi* who is a protector of the forest and a hunter. He is often depicted as a friend or ally of both the *caboclos* (rural dwellers, often mixed race) and the nature spirits of the forests. The plant and the god are seen as friendly beings who feed the local populace. In both the song and the myth narrated at the beginning of the chapter, the *açaí* palm is anthropomorphized in interesting ways. The myth attributes the origin of the tree to a buried child. In this way it descends from local people and supports their well-being. The red juice of the fruit is symbolically associated with blood and health. This song refers to the island of Marajó, which is a large island in the middle of the Amazon River near its mouth. It describes *açaí* as the taste of Marajó, thus attributing a particular *terroir* to the fruit grown on this island. Much *açaí* is grown on this island and today much of it is prepared for export here.

As mentioned earlier, many people feel that "without *açaí* I am still hungry" (Sigueira 2010). In this way, *açaí*, like manioc, symbolizes a relation with a food that transcends its mere nutritive properties and embodies the essence of "food" in the same way that rice does for many Asian cultures, and potato does for many central European cultures. It defines an occasion as a meal and not just a snack.

Many people also have a discriminating sense of *terroir* in relation to *açaí*, preferring the product of one region over another. Nowadays, as I have mentioned, people complain that the taste of the *açaí* is changing as the methods of production also change, from small riverine holdings to large plantation stands of the palms that are often far inland from the river and the traditional modes of cultivation. These connoisseurs see a change in the quality of the product. Although the local population does not use the term *terroir* to discuss the qualities of the fruit, restaurateurs and researchers are now applying the term (Sigueira 2010). Although the *açaí* market in Belém, and in some other large Amazonian towns, is still thriving, much of the fruit harvested is processed elsewhere rather than sold fresh. Although small-scale pulp and juice producers have catered to locals in the *Ver-o-Peso* market for years, the bulk of the processing has now moved to large plants that freeze and dry the majority of the fruit for long-term preservation and far-flung markets.

Although *açaí* is a fruit in any classification, it holds a special position apart from other fruits and has to be treated slightly differently. One cannot eat *açaí* in combination with certain other vegetable foods, such as *tacacá* (see Chapter 3) for fear that the different components will not combine properly and will instead cause a stomachache. In addition, *açaí* cannot be eaten in conjunction with other kinds of fruit; it must be eaten alone (Sigueira 2010). This local belief differs significantly from the practice outside of Pará and the Amazon of making juices and smoothies that mix *açaí* with multiple other fruits, particularly blueberry and pomegranate, or serving it frozen with bananas and granola.

Açaí is usually served in Pará as a soup or porridge with *farinha* and sugar and can be eaten as either a savory or a sweet dish. It is not traditionally served as a sorbet with bananas and granola, nor as a health food drink, although it can be served as a juice. As *açaí* becomes more globalized, however, its meaning changes and with those changes come new ways of serving it. In the South and Northeast, *açaí* is primarily served as a *vitamina* (energy drink) or as a *gelada*, or sorbet, which is served in a bowl with slices of fruit around the sides and granola sprinkled on top. This way of serving it is very popular, especially with tourists, but in Pará the locals are very suspicious of consuming *açaí* with these pairings and can be aggressively defensive about how to eat their dish. When I walked past a market snack bar that had a sign in front of it announcing the availability of *açaí*, I called out to the *barraquieiro*, "Oh, you have *açaí*!" He quickly responded in a somewhat surly fashion, "We don't serve it with bananas and granola, it's just plain *açaí*." When I responded, "Plain? Don't you serve *farinha* with it?" his tone changed dramatically, and he said, "Oh yes! We serve *farinha* and sugar." His original antagonism was directed toward me as a foreigner and a tourist, one who was acquainted with *açaí* from other parts of the country and expected to find that dish served in Belém. When I showed that I knew the local way of eating the dish, his manner changed and became more inclusive and friendly, implying that we shared a respect for the local food. I transcended the "mere tourist" category and became a knowledgeable foreigner. The exchange illustrates how the Paraense differentiate insiders from outsiders. Insiders eat *açaí* in the traditional way and appreciate the local customs. Outsiders have adopted this food and transformed it, using it in what Paraenses feel are inappropriate ways that "disrespect" the local value of the food. A relatively new chain of restaurants opening in Belém plays to both these audiences. *Point de Açaí* has three locales and is

growing. It serves classic *açaí* pulp with *chapas* (griddles or planks) of assorted fish
or meats. Along with these dishes, the establishment serves a pitcher of *açaí*, a large
shaker of *tapioca*, and another of *farinha*. Sugar sits on the table. Further along the
menu, however, is the *açaí na tigela*, the frozen bowl of *açaí* served with bananas
and granola. This restaurant seemed popular with both locals and foreigners.

Although the *barraqueiros* in the Paraense markets remain faithful to the traditional way of serving the dish and catered to a predominantly local clientele, the
fancier restaurants in town are concurrently experimenting with new ways of fixing
and presenting the fruit. I saw ice creams, tarts, cakes, custard, and sorbets made with
açaí. Even the most famous Paraense chef, Paulo Martins, owner and chef of *Lá en
Casa*, a nationally known restaurant, has created a *pudim de açaí* made with eggs,
sugar, and condensed milk (Martins 2005). Another recipe describes a *mousse de
açaí* that can be decorated with either meringue or *tapioca* (Bosisio 2000; Trevisani
2002; Martins 2005). This process of combining traditional foods in recipes more
frequently used for traditional European or American dishes is becoming a great deal
more popular across the country and will be discussed in Chapter 6.

Açaí is touted as Amazonian, and as I said above, has been codified as a trademark
of the State of Pará. In Belém, in particular, consuming *açaí* creates a bond with a
place; there is a local saying, *Quem vai a Pará parou, tomou açaí ficou* ("Those who
come to Pará and eat/drink *açaí* will stay").[5] This ditty can be found on T-shirts and
tea towels and asserts the maxim that drinking *açaí* makes you Paraense. What we
eat helps form our identity as instantiated by the famous quote from Brillat-Savarin:
Dites-moi ce que te manges, et je te dis ce que tu es ("Tell me what you eat, and I
will tell you who you are") (Brillat-Savarin [1825] 2011). Eating *açaí* thus produces
a certain type of person, subjectivity, or identity that associates one with the region,
in fact it holds or binds one to the region. This identity as a Paraense may be rooted
in one's birth and residence in the region, but it is maintained in large part through
a person's relation to the land, and the food and drink it provides. Paraenses build
their identities through continual connection to this patrimony. They are absorbing
the "taste of place" and embodying the *terroir* of the region (cf. Trubek 2008). Those
who arrive in Pará as outsiders, without this shared substance can make themselves
Paraense by sharing the same food. By eating Paraense food, they embody the essence of Pará. *Açaí* is the food that builds this identity most strongly. Although the
motto on the T-shirt expresses this value, the process is more complicated and can
even be fraught with antagonism. The crux of this complexity is that it is not just the
raw fruit, *açaí*, that creates a certain kind of identity but the context as well as how
it is served that matters. To Paraense residents, eating *açaí* daily with the proper accompaniments of *tapioca* or *farinha* is the authentic way.

One reason why *açaí* plays such an important role in local identity is its tendency
to induce lethargy. According to locals like the premier Paraense chef, Paulo Martins, *açaí* is a heavy food that weighs you down and makes you lethargic and sleepy.
It enacts its local roots by rooting those who consume it to the place. For this reason,

according to Martins (2009), you have to be careful when you serve it. He suggests it should only be served when the diners can relax or have a siesta after the meal, Saturday or Sunday midday meals being the most preferred. Of course, while such beliefs exist in the general population, those who depend on *açaí* as a staple food do not always have the luxury to rest after consuming it since they may consume it for every meal. This local value of heaviness offers an explanation of why *açaí* is believed to root people to the locale so that if you drink it you will settle in Pará. In a recent article in the *New York Times*, author Seth Kugel was surprised to find this belief in the soporific qualities of *açaí* to be widespread across the region (2010).

These beliefs about the deenergizing properties of *açaí*, however, contradict the quickly globalizing and increasingly celebrated popular view of *açaí* as an energizing food. Here we find a distinct difference between the local and the global. The beliefs held outside of Pará are detached from the local culture and the local contexts of kinship, family, and household consumption. Martins (2009) does not like this paradoxical disconnect and would like the rest of the world to appreciate the local values.

Moving beyond the Amazon

The belief that *açaí* is an energizing agent has become lodged in the collective consciousness of Brazilians in the country's South. Here, *açaí* is considered a *vitamina*, or health drink. It is served as a juice in health clubs, at juice bars, and on the beach where volleyball players and surfers consume it.[6] As a source for energy and vitality, *açaí* is considered highly nutritive. The downside of this reputation is that it is believed to be highly caloric and therefore taboo to calorie-conscious Brazilians despite its nutritive properties. Most women immediately told me they do not eat or drink *açaí* because it is so high in calories and very fattening. Much of the calorie count may be due to the sweeteners used to improve the flavor. My Brazilian friends, however, denied this rationale and believed that *açaí* is intrinsically more caloric than other foods. Of course, its very nutritive and caloric properties are what endear it to the people who depend on it as a staple food. In the South, however, its association with athletes and with the ability to reenergize them gives it a masculine and muscular association. As elsewhere, it has certain qualities that are associated with the body, but this tends to be the body of male athletes and not of any particular regional identity. It is not perceived as a regional food but is perceived as a "gendered" food.

A second aspect that has come to be associated with *açaí* is its popularity as a frozen snack or dessert. In towns and cities in Bahia, Rio, São Paulo, and Minas Gerais, frozen *açaí* is a common snack or dessert. In cafes and snack bars a bowl of this frozen dessert (it is called *açaí na tigela*, or "*açaí* in a bowl") is commonly served with sliced bananas and sprinkled with granola. It is very popular with tourists, especially European and American youth and women tourists. The masculine associations of the sports drink are replaced by the exotic and refreshing characteristics of the frozen dish that appeals to women as a healthy snack. When queried, most of my Bahian

Figure 4.3   *Açaí na tigela*—chilled *açaí* served in a bowl with bananas and granola. Photograph by Jane Fajans.

friends claimed that they did not like *açaí* but commented on how all the tourists did. It had no local connotations for them, and they classified the taste as sour and gritty. While Bahians did not know where *açaí* came from, most of the tourists did and strongly associated it with the Amazon.

Another shift in the consumption of *açaí* outside the region is the addition of *guaraná* to the frozen pulp. Many of the snack bars and stands that sell *açaí na tigela* also add *guaraná* to the mix. Since *guaraná* contains a lot of a caffeine-like chemical, it is no wonder the dish is thought to be energizing. This recipe again differs from the practices in Pará and other parts of the Amazon where *açaí* is not supposed to be consumed with other fruits.

The irony of this treatment of *açaí* is that the value of food shifts once again from the rooted and somewhat soporific food of the Amazon, through the gendered properties of the food as an energizing *vitamina* consumed mostly by men, to the tasty, refreshing, and exotic snack enjoyed by many foreign women (and some men) who believe it to have health-giving properties.

Beyond Brazil

Instead of the locally embedded meanings described above, outside of Brazil *açaí* takes on the amplified symbolic "natural" properties of the region from whence it comes, the Amazon. *Açaí* has become a faddish health food in the Euro-American diet. It is one of several tropical fruits that have been deemed "superfoods" because of their health properties. From Oprah Winfrey to Rachel Ray, in *Men's Fitness* magazine, and on numerous websites, *açaí* has been touted as a miracle cure-all.[7] The properties attributed to this fruit are myriad and many of them contrast with the properties that the food has in Pará. As in Southern Brazil, *açaí* is viewed as a health food, but in Euro-America its energy-inducing properties are combined with claims of antiaging, weight loss, and detoxifying properties. The claims that it enables fabulous weight loss have headed the list of benefits attributed to this food. Paradoxically, this claim is most at odds with the belief in its nutritive and caloric properties that hold so firmly in Brazil.

Several websites claim *açaí* contains more antioxidants than most or all of the leading antioxidant-rich fruits such as blueberries and red grapes. One advertisement claimed "No other berry or fruit product can come close to matching the nutritional and antioxidant content of *Açaí*" (Anon. 2006).

In the United States, current marketing efforts by retail merchants and Internet businesses suggest *açaí* products can help consumers lose weight, lower cholesterol, gain energy, prevent and/or cure cancer, improve muscle tone, and solve digestive problems. The juice of this fruit was touted on Oprah Winfrey's and Rachael Ray's shows among others, and the many websites that sell *açaí* powder, juice, and other Amazonian products all cited Oprah's promotion despite the fact she has now repudiated it (Colapinto 2011).

On August 19, 2009, Harpo, Inc., producers of *The Oprah Winfrey Show* and *The Dr. Oz Show*, along with Dr. Mehmet Oz, filed a trademark infringement complaint against 40 Internet marketers of dietary supplements, including acai berry products among others. Neither Ms. Winfrey nor Dr. Oz has ever sponsored or endorsed any acai berry, resveratrol, colon cleanse or dietary supplement product. (*Açaí* 2011a)

The seemingly endless miraculous attributes claimed on behalf of *açaí* are exemplified by the following excerpt.

A synergy of monounsaturated (healthy) fats, dietary fiber and phytosterols to help promote cardiovascular and digestive health. It is thought to be an almost perfect essential amino acid complex in conjunction with valuable trace minerals, vital to proper muscle contraction and regeneration. (*Açaí* 2011c)

Additional studies purport to show that *açaí*'s energy is principally derived from fat consisting of unsaturated fatty acids. These acids contain a highly active substance that circulates in the blood and works to eliminate the saturated fatty acids (which cause vein or artery obstruction).

These are just a fraction of the claims that have multiplied across the health community. The fruit is touted as a detoxicant, an antiaging tonic, a heart protector, a bone strengthener, an immune booster, and an anticancer agent, in addition to its weight loss and energy properties. On top of these qualities, *açaí* is claimed to be rich in fibers that help the digestive system.

Despite such enthusiastic pronouncements, many sources remind the potential user that "A lot of claims are being made, but most of them haven't been tested scientifically. We are just beginning to understand the complexity of the *Açaí* berry and its health-promoting effects" (*Açaí* 2011a). Contemporary web searches combine multiple articles about the "myth" of *açaí* and the repudiation of the health claims so avidly promoted just a few years ago with the continued promotion of these claims with heightened references to scientific evidence. The jury is still out on many of these claims that science validates the attributes of this product. Despite this, the popularity of this and other superfoods persists and grows.

Transcending the Regional

Açaí is in a sense two foods now: the local ingredient that has historic and mythic properties and represents an embodied rootedness in the local environment; and the exported fruit that is viewed as a superfood and miracle drug, its food properties greatly undervalued. Many people outside of Pará consume *açaí* not for its taste or social values, but for its nutritive properties; a number of these consumers actually do not like the taste, they find it muddy and gritty-tasting and add significant amounts of sugar to make it more palatable. Each group of consumers has a sense of the meaning of the food in their own context, but neither understands the value and identity the other imputes to the food. In fact, most of the world is ignorant of the local uses and values of the fruit and has coopted the fruit for its own globalized uses. Meanwhile Paraenses are trying hard to hold on to this important resource in the way they have always known and used it. In this, they feel increasingly vulnerable as the fruit has become scarcer and more expensive locally.

The difference between these two understandings of *açaí*, however, is shaped not just by the fruit itself but by the context in which the fruit is grown and harvested and the attitudes the different groups have toward that environment. These differences coincide with two very different images of the Amazon region itself. The Amazon is, on the one hand, a geographic region of Brazil (and six other countries) rich in natural resources such as energy, minerals, and land. On the other hand, it is also a vast region of exotic and "virgin" forest valued primarily for its natural floral and faunal properties. These notions of economic riches and connotations of pristine nature inform the imagery used to promote both tourism in the Amazon and the products derived from the region.

From afar, *açaí* fills the stereotype of an exotic and natural product. Like many fruits it is eaten in a relatively natural state (peeled and puréed, or dried and powered) and thus directly instantiates the health and vitality of this region. *Açaí* thus readily takes on the symbolic properties of the locale in which it grows. This has widely been taken to imply that by eating *açaí* or *cupuaçu* (to take another popular fruit touted as having multiple health benefits) one can embody this natural vitality of the Amazon and all its health-giving properties. The claim of its proponents that it has been "scientifically shown" to be naturally healthful and curative in so many ways bolsters this image. Here, Western knowledge is superimposed on indigenous regional perceptions to create a food that is a multivocalic symbol of otherness to the European and American consumer.

One of these associations has to do with sustainability. *Açaí* has become not only a symbol of nature, but also an icon of sustainable production. NGOs and websites tout the fact that *açaí* is produced by small-scale producers in harmony with their surroundings. Although not promoted as a "fair trade" commodity, it is presumed to be produced in a socially responsible way both for the producers and as an organic product. Neither of these assumptions is made explicit, in part because of the prevailing sentiments surrounding the Amazon and the sense that indigenous fruits are in harmony in ways that other commodity production is not (cattle, soy, etc.). The producers of *açaí* themselves are represented as partaking of the naturalness of the environment in which they reside.

Other Superfoods

Açaí is not the only product of the Amazon to benefit from this symbolic combination of healthy properties and ecological associations. There is a growing number of such products. In particular, *guaraná* and *cupuaçu* have become valued members of the new category of superfoods, or nutriceuticals (foods valued for their healthy as well as nutritive properties). *Cupuaçu* is a fruit that grows on a tree. Some proponents say it is as healthy or healthier than *açaí* and has the added benefit that it is easier to grow without destroying the forest (*Açaí* 2011b). It thus avoids the tension over the increasing association of *açaí* with the new commercial plantations being carved out of the forest to meet the growing global demand for their fruit. This claim makes it more sustainable than *açaí*.

> *Açaí* has been available in certain sectors of the health food community for half a dozen years. Recently, *Cupuaçu* fruit has become touted as the latest "superfruit." In fact, *cupuaçu* is considered the most promising of all fruits from the lush Amazon. It is a member of the Cocoa family and has a prized exotic taste, combining elements of chocolate, bananas and passion fruit. (*Açaí* 2011b)

The ingredients to which these effects are attributed include phytonutrient polyphenols, vitamins B_1, B_2, and B_3, and at least nine antioxidants. Several corporations have begun production of *cupuaçu*-based food supplements including pills, drinks, smoothies, and sweets that are trumpeted on multiple websites. The white pulp of the *cupuaçu* is uniquely fragrant (described as a mix of chocolate and pineapple). It is frequently used in desserts, juices, ice creams, and sweets in Pará, but it is only available in powdered form outside the country.

On the *Today* show, Andrew Zimmern of the Travel Channel described *cupuaçu* as "the pharmacy of the Amazon" (Zimmern 2009). According to him, the populations that have been eating and cultivating *cupuaçu* for generations look to the plant for a variety of medical applications. *Cupuaçu* is often used as a painkiller. It purportedly provides antioxidants and other benefits to the digestive system. In addition, the theobromides in *cupuaçu* are believed to act like caffeine to provide energy and alertness. Additional claims assert it is also able to lower cholesterol and increase male potency. Finally, *cupuaçu* is often sold as a lotion or cream because it has rejuvenating effects on the skin (www.cupuacu.com/).

Conclusions

The attraction of these superfoods resides as much in their symbolic association with a rich, healthy part of the world as it does in the so-called proven empirical qualities attributed to them. They are enticing because they embody symbolic properties of health, unspoiled nature, and a simpler way of life, all of which can be conveyed to the consumer in a drink or lotion, sorbet or smoothie. Those who buy and consume these products do so to improve themselves as healthy, active beings but also to bolster their self-identity as actors who support sustainability and fair trade exchanges. In a quest to partake of all the best that the world has to offer, consumers in the First World fall prey to these images and a fantasy of a world beyond their own. That the actual world from which these substances come is vastly different from their fantasy only occasionally penetrates the consciousness of the consumers.

To the residents of the Amazon, both in the cities and small villages and towns along the river and its tributaries, the Amazon is a productive and constructed environment. Although people live off the rich resources of the environment, they know that these resources need cultivation and transformation. Even the *açaí* fruit needs to be planted and harvested. Other foodstuffs require even more labor and social investment. The production and consumption of Amazonian foods are imbued with the embedded meanings of these diverse social and cultural groups. These meanings are not reduced to the pristine natural properties of the locale but are entwined with family, regional, cultural, and linguistic symbols that impart value to the substances produced from it by their labor, such as *açaí, cupuaçu, guaraná*, and others. The social context in which people share and consume the products also contributes their meanings and values to the regional inhabitants. These social and cultural values remain rooted in the region itself; they do not get passed along to those who consume the food beyond its borders. This disconnect is why local people resent the cooptation of their food by the wider world and seek to keep it firmly tied to their way of life. The market vendors in the *Ver-o-Peso* market in Belém uphold the traditional ways of eating *açaí* and defend it against the new ways that outsiders have learned and expect to find in the local market stalls, giving rise to resentment from the *barraqueiros*. Local chefs and others involved in the changing gastronomic scene are more likely to experiment with fusion or innovative recipes and dishes, but even they cleave emotionally to the traditional ways. Despite this wish to retain control over the meanings and values of foods such as *açaí*, the processes of globalization have become too dominant to succumb to such desires. More and more the foods we find in our stores and restaurants are depersonalized, detached, and often denuded of even a place of origin (Wilk 2006). We learn what is in our foods, but only rarely do we know from whence they came. In this regard, it is interesting that *açaí* has so richly retained its connection to the Amazon and its exotic appeal to those so far away.

"Home Cooking" from the Heartland: The *Comida Caseira* of Minas Gerais

Despite Brazil's large size and many subregions, national attitudes toward food span the country. Brazilians celebrate food and extol its plentitude. Food should be *comida farta* ("satisfying and filling"); there should be a lot of food for a large number of people. These descriptions may suggest that Brazilians value quantity over quality. That conclusion would be erroneous; instead, *comida farta* suggests well-being due to repletion, while care taken over the preparation of food is also highly valued. To many Brazilians who talked to me about food this way, *farta* connotes an experience of well-being, security, and the good life.

The national staples of rice and beans are the easiest and most common way to achieve these ideals. As most nutritionists know, rice and beans are complementary foods that provide the basic amino acids for a healthy diet. Although rice and beans are parts of the diet throughout the country, they are less pervasive in the Amazon than elsewhere (see Chapters 3 and 4). Outside of the Amazon, people may eat these foods at least twice a day, and ideally they will eat a piece of meat, chicken, or fish with them. The average Brazilian eats a lunch that consists of rice, beans, *farinha*, meat, and macaroni, commonly and fondly referred to as a PF or *prato feito* ("prepared plate"). This dish is served in restaurants, street stalls, and bus stations, and is reproduced at home when people come home for lunch. Friends and informants, speaking in general terms about Brazilian foods, usually remark on how ubiquitous rice and beans are and how they are the mainstay of every diet. They also joke about their love of big meals.

A focus on plentitude and repletion is easy to understand in a country and culture in which hunger and scarcity have been common for a large percentage of the population at least until recently. As in the case of European "peasant" dishes, Brazilian *comida caseira* is frequently of the type that emerges from the need to feed many mouths with limited resources. In Brazil, the dishes that have emerged in this context have several interwoven histories. In the early days of Portuguese colonization, the settlers were not as inclined to farming and homesteading as they were in North America. Many were there primarily to explore and exploit (Burns 1993: 47; Skidmore 2010: 32; Vianna Moog 1964). In this vein, they tended to depend heavily on the foods they could obtain from the local native population. These earlier colonists depended on manioc, *açaí*, and fish. As such, much of this diet became rooted in the foodways of later arrivals. Later arrivals brought some of their own foodstuffs and many of their own cooking techniques. Local foods became intertwined with dishes from Europe (especially Portugal), Africa, India, Japan, Germany, Italy, Lebanon, and Russia, among others. This evolution is still continuing as new populations arrive, share, and adapt. The number of such mixtures is too great to enumerate, but examples include mango sushi, French fried *macaxeira*, pizza with various tropical fruits, and bean and meat stews of all varieties. Despite this variety, home cooking is still based on rice and beans. Over time rice has become an increasingly large percentage of the diet because, as people told me, it is so cheap.

Comida Caseira

Comida caseira means "home cooking" and evokes the quintessential comfort food of childhood and day-to-day meals. The Brazilian cuisine most recognized as *comida caseira* is Mineiran food (from the state of Minas Gerais), although many of the attributes inherent in Mineiran food are shared with neighboring regions. This is comfort food par excellence. As elsewhere in the country, Mineiran food combines the flavors and ingredients of Europe (primarily Portugal), Africa, and Native America. The array of ingredients and the feel of the dishes are reminiscent of Caribbean specialties and American Soul Food and have a similar appeal and a similar origin. Mineiran food makes much use of pork (in all its forms from crackling to sausage, bacon, and roasts), beans, and cooked leafy greens (often prepared with pork fat). This food is recognized as emblematic of the "heart of the nation" while also being the food that is found around the country. As the heart of the nation, Minas is one of the oldest states and has a long colonial history. Many Mineirans have historically emigrated to other parts of Brazil and the world; as these flows of people have moved and spread, they have also widely disseminated Mineiran culture and foods. Mineiran restaurants can be found throughout the country and abroad. Although no longer considered so healthy, Mineiran cuisine was for many years considered the quintessential *comida caseira.*

Although much home cooking shares features with Mineiran food, the content of *comida caseira* varies across regions; there is no uniform Brazilian "home cooking." Despite the obvious truth of this fact, and the evidence described in this book, the food of Minas Gerais has come to represent home cooking across the nation and in the eyes of foreigners. Many factors contribute to this perception. While not literally or geographically central to Brazil, Minas is an inland state far from the coast and the national frontiers. As Mineirans (people from Minas Gerais) migrated to other parts of Brazil to work in the cities, and more particularly, as domestic workers in the homes of middle-class and wealthy residents, they introduced the cuisine they knew and loved. In this way, much of the rest of the country has grown up eating this food and associating it with all the comforts and nostalgia of home. For many, rice and beans, bean stews, and pork dishes of all kinds have taken on the affective connotations of comfort food and the food of childhood. The *prato feito* condenses this affect into a readily accessible meal. Nowhere is this emphasis on abundance and satisfaction based on combinations of humble ingredients more evident than in the food of Minas Gerais.

Minas, as its name implies, was a center for mining of a large array of precious metals and stones. The labor in the mines was primarily done by African slaves. Minas has had, from the start, a very large Afro-Brazilian population relative to its total population. While much of the culture retains this legacy, Mineiran food more than another regional cuisine embodies what we (North Americans) think of as Soul Food: beans, greens, and bits of pork.

Mineiran Food as Soul Food

As Peter Fry wrote in 1977, Brazilian food and American Soul Food are very similar. This similarity is due, in large part, to a shared history of the African diaspora. Fry clarifies that beyond a shared history of their African origin, these kindred traditions share centuries of slavery and the subsequent years of poverty and discrimination. Across the African diaspora, the descendants of African slaves have created foods out of two sources: the foods they brought over from Africa (or their New World equivalents—roots, greens, flours, and oils), which they planted in small plots of unused and marginal land; and the leftovers and residue from the kitchens of the wealthy (Mintz 1996; Hughes 1991). For this reason, we find variants on pork and beans, collard greens and grits, in many places in the Western Hemisphere. What strikes Fry and others is the way that much of this African/slave heritage became embedded in the national culture of Brazil whereas it remains very particularly ethnic and regional in the United States (Fry 1977; Harris 1992; Hughes 1991; Mintz 1996). Although combined in a variety of different forms, these foods form the basis of Mineiran cooking. They also contain the basis of what has become essentially generic Brazilian cooking. Mineiran food can use the label "home cooking" (*comida caseira*) without raising eyebrows, even if not all Brazilians eat it on a regular basis.

Mineiran food does not contain the more exotic ingredients of African origin we discussed in the chapter on Bahia such as *dendê* oil or coconut milk, or the rich legacy of Amazonian food such as *tucupi* or *açaí*, or the special *cerrado* ingredients such as *piqui*[1] (prominent in the foods of neighboring Goias). Mineiran food retains the simple, filling properties of a peasant diet and comfort food. The food of Minas, as stated above, is also the cuisine most related to many of the other African diaspora cuisines, focusing on pork, beans, rice, okra, and greens. Many of these dishes are made with skimpy pieces of lower-end cuts of pork (ears, tail, snout, feet, and organs), reminiscent of the Soul Food/Southern style of cooking. As with Soul Food, the cuisine uses these cheaper, less valued cuts to create food that satisfies the soul. The meat is primarily used to flavor the beans, and the beans are most frequently used to flavor the rice, mixed up with rice either in a pot or on the plate. These staples are accompanied by okra or finely shredded collard greens or related leafy greens that are sautéed with garlic and olive oil (see recipe in Chapter 6 for *couve*).

Mineiran Food as Peasant Food

Mineiran food is both uniquely a kind of Soul Food and concurrently a transformation of European peasant food. Food from this region is frequently made in a casserole and slow cooked (as opposed to the relatively rapid cooking methods of Bahian food). These dishes contain a combination of meats, vegetables, and starches. Beans (predominantly black but some dishes have other varieties) are the principal starch featured in these dishes, while the principal greens used are okra or *couve*, a leafy green similar to collard greens. The casseroles that are the specialty of the region are made of soapstone that keeps a low, even heat and maintains that heat for a long time. This cooking method resembles that of the European peasant dishes of meat and beans, or meat and potatoes, often cooked in the still-warm bread ovens of the village bakeries, a tradition that was also carried over to parts of Brazil.

Mineiran dishes that resemble European ones are *frango ao molho pardo* (chicken with dark sauce, cooked in its own blood), *galinhada* (a chicken fricassee), *feijão tropeiro* (trooper's beans), and the cheese *catupiri* (a mild cow's milk cheese).

The preparation and ingredients of the dishes differ on either side of the Atlantic, but they are close enough to suggest that they are the product of migration back and forth across the ocean. This migration was probably not a one-time occurrence but comprised several different flows of people, each with its own recipes and ingredients. Perhaps this is why these foods seem so familiar to visitors to Brazil. Although they may not have the same beans, greens, or even starches, they have what could be called cognate versions of these ingredients. The bean dishes are reminiscent of French, Portuguese, and Spanish dishes, but the Brazilians substitute chicken, turkey, or duck for goose or rabbit. In Portugal one finds numerous dishes with the same names as Brazilian dishes, Portuguese *feijoada*, *cozida*, *frango com molho pardo*, and *peixada*, and these all share "cognate" ingredients.

Rice and Beans

The rice and beans combination, so prevalent across much of the Caribbean and Latin American world, underscores most meals in Brazil too, although the rice and beans are not considered a single dish. They are not cooked together as they are in many of the countries in the vicinity. Despite this separation, rice and beans are so strongly intertwined that they are referred to as "the perfect couple." This designation refers to both the nutritional and the symbolic aspects of the complementary foods (Barbosa 2012). On the one hand they are as ordinary as any basic staple, and they can be metaphors for the mundane and boring; one can refer to rice and beans much as one can use the expression "bread and butter" in English to refer to something basic but necessary and taken-for-granted. Idioms referring to rice and beans are widespread in the language (Barbosa 2012; Doría 2012) and make it clear that they are the foods that provide comfort and satisfaction. Nutritionally, rice and beans are recognized as having a perfect complement of nutrients, especially amino acids, so that together they provide a sound diet. In this sense, too, they are the perfect couple. The government branch that promotes agriculture and husbandry in Brazil, EMBRAPA, has just published a book called *The Perfect Couple* (2011) about rice and beans.

In addition to symbolizing the everyday, and the value of complementarity—be it in marriage or in nutrition—rice and beans are symbolically used to refer to the racial differences that are prevalent in Brazil. Rice is white and beans are black or red (called *mulatinho*, which translates as *mulatto* or "mixed race") and together they mix just like Brazilians (Barbosa 2012). This symbolic association has gained a new cogency in recent years as agricultural experts have rediscovered the fact that the rice grown predominantly in Brazil is of African origin. The beans are indigenous, so the combination of the two is also part of the melding of these cultures, continents, and history. Another symbolic pairing attributed to rice and beans is the humeral one of hot and cold, dry and moist foods. Beans are considered a hot food, while rice is classified as cold (Doría 2012).

Rice and beans are so ubiquitous in the Brazilian diet that they become one of the foods that people miss most when they leave the country. Numerous expatriates mentioned how they were suddenly confirmed rice-and-bean eaters even when they had not been so at home. Some of them even seem quite surprised at this discovery about themselves.

Home Cooking

Residents of Minas have migrated across Brazil into all major urban areas and northward to Mexico and the United States. They have carried their cuisine with them and have made it popular wherever they go. Many of the migrants have worked as domestic help and cooks in the cities of São Paulo and Rio, and thus this cuisine has come to represent everyday food in many households in these cities. During my first trip to Brazil, we "house sat" an apartment and retained the services of the Mineiran *empregada* (domestic worker) employed by the owners. She continued to cook for us and prepared food in the Mineiran culinary repertoire. Our daily meals conformed to the pattern of rice, beans, a piece of meat, usually pork, and a green. We also ate similar meals at friends' houses. My view of Brazilian food was framed in this pattern until I went to Bahia (see Chapter 2).

Figure 5.1   The full array of dishes at a Mineiran buffet. Photograph by Jane Fajans.

Even more revealing about the pervasiveness of Mineiran food is the fact that every city and practically every *Shopping* (shopping mall) has a restaurant called something like *Comida Mineira, Mineira Caseira, Coração Mineira,* or *Comida Caseira* ("Mineiran Food," "Mineiran Home," "the Mineiran Heart," or just "Home Cooking"). Such restaurants offer large buffets for either a single price, or *a quilo* (by weight). These restaurants are typically decorated with red-checked tablecloths, staff wearing gingham skirts or aprons, and pottery or soapstone serving dishes to underscore the symbols of home, food, and heart (or heartland), which enhance their appeal. Restaurant signs promote their offerings as home cooking, made with love, or as cooking from the heart (also a play on "heartland," a position that Minas Gerais holds for many).

The buffets contain a vast array of dishes, but within this plentitude, there are certain invariable themes: several bean dishes; numerous variations on okra, chard, kale, and other forms of greens; multiple varieties of sausage; *carne do sol*, rice, and vegetables; *farofas*, potatoes, pastas, and meats (either stewed or freshly grilled). Desserts consist of fresh fruits (often as fruit salads) or fruit compotes of sweetened preserved fruits in syrup or in the form of thick fruit pastes, which are served with Minas cheese. This Mineiran cheese is ubiquitous at breakfast tables around the country, but it is also served as a dessert, most commonly in combination with a thick fruit paste made from guavas (*goiabada*). The combination of sweet and salty is colloquially called *Romeo e Julieta*. From this panoply of food in a restaurant, a customer can select foods to create a *prato feito* composed of the familiar comfort foods, or experiment and sample new and different dishes. The overall effect, however, is abundance and satisfaction.

At such establishments, one finds business and working people eating lunch, now that the practice of returning home for the midday meal has lost out to the exigencies of the business day and the increasing need to commute to work. On vacations, weekends, or when retired, many people revert to the prolonged midday meal of earlier centuries. The evening meal then becomes a light supper (*lanche* or snack), or a bigger meal that is eaten later in the evening (often quite late). I remember a party where the meal was served at 3:00 A.M. (a practice one can still find in Portugal), although this was extreme in my Brazilian experience.

The pattern of eating a large midday meal is known to us as a remnant of the farm life of earlier eras, but it has persisted in urban life in Brazil because of the pattern of domestic help. The large midday meal fits with the schedule of daily domestic workers who can shop, cook, and clean up before leaving at sundown, often leaving a light *lanche* for the family for supper. In several families I stayed with, I watched the *empregadas* start cooking in the morning. They usually served the food as a midday meal. The families never ate more than bread and sandwiches in the evening unless they went out with friends to a restaurant meal. Those unable to eat at home often eat at one of the *a quilo* buffets mentioned above that offer a buffet with an assortment of meats, beans, greens, and sweets. However, fancier restaurants with menus and table service are also popular for the wealthier or more leisured diners.

Preparing a Meal

Many, if not most, Brazilian dishes begin with the frying of garlic in olive oil. The streets and alleyways (the areas closest to the kitchens situated at the back of many houses) are pungent with the smell of garlic and oil in the hours preceding meals. To this day, the smell of garlic frying in oil evokes in me the sensory memory of the anticipation of a Brazilian meal. Although this savory combination of food and smells is common to many Mediterranean cuisines, it somehow feels even more embedded in Brazilian gastronomy, even though the taste of garlic is not overly prominent in most of the dishes that start out with this base.

The second major component of cooking in a Brazilian household generally begins with the washing and soaking of a large pot of dried beans. Several hours later, the beans are cooked, either in a pressure cooker, which saves time and fuel, or more slowly in a big pot. The beans are cooked until tender but not mushy, and then may be eaten immediately or set aside for later use, up to two or three days later since a big pot may be prepared at one time. The beans soften and become creamier over time. The beans are then mixed with olive oil, garlic, and onion (and maybe some other vegetables like peppers, tomatoes, and cilantro). Often the broth from the beans is drunk separately as a soup, *caldo*, before a meal. Sometimes, the broth is mixed back into the beans to make them creamier. Both the beans and the rice, which almost universally accompanies it, are begun with garlic and oil, and often a bit of onion. Meats such as steaks or chops are usually simply fried or grilled, but certain parts are stewed in the beans after being parboiled. They thus flavor the beans.

Caldo

One of the most common foods eaten at home, often for supper, is *caldo*. *Caldo* is soup or broth, eaten in a relaxed and intimate way. The simplest *caldo* is the broth from the beans (mentioned above). Other varieties are made of corn, chicken, or vegetables. This soup is medium thick and mostly puréed. The excess liquid from a *feijoada* is often poured off and served as *caldo* in a bowl or mug on the side. Originally, *caldo* was the base or broth from which other soups or stews were fashioned, but the term is now used for the final product of a simple meal. *Caldo* is served with some standard condiments, usually one or two slices of bread, a small portion of shredded cheese, several slices of sausage, and sometimes a garnish of green onions. *Caldo* is served both at home and in restaurants, but as restaurant food its popularity varies greatly from one region to another. In Minas and the neighboring state of Goias, many restaurants, food stalls, and small storefronts advertise that they have *caldo* with signs out front stating "*Temos caldo*" ("We have *caldo*"). In Goias, *caldo* is often advertised along with *pamonha*, a tamale-like food of cornmeal steamed in a corn husk (it may have a filling of cheese or sweet paste, or just be plain or slightly sweetened) that is popular during festivals like *São João*, and *empada* or *empadão* (large *empada*), a pastry filled with shredded meat, usually chicken that is baked not fried (the fried version of this is called a *pastel*). These savory snack foods go under the heading of *salgado*. The small bars and restaurants that serve this food are basically late-night eateries, open from 9:00 P.M. until they run out around 1:00 A.M.

Caldos and *salgado* snacks are popular take-out foods for Saturday or Sunday supper after a large midday meal such as *feijoada*. Although *caldo* is available in other parts of the country, it does not have the same popular cachet and is not as prevalent as I found it to be in Minas and Goias. For most of the country, *caldo* remains a food eaten for supper, often in the kitchen, and one that has a nostalgic connotation of childhood.

When I asked a friend, over a bowl of such broth, to define the difference between soup (*sopa*) and *caldo* (broth or creamy soup), she was confused and could not readily answer me, but finally volunteered that the real difference in her mind was the kind of bowl it was served in. *Caldo*, she suggested, was served in a mug or small bowl (*tigela*) and soup was served in a soup bowl (*prato de sopa*). The use of the bowl or mug makes it more intimate and homey. Another friend defined the difference as referring to whether the soup was smooth or had bits and pieces in it, the latter being soup and the former *caldo*. These are not dictionary definitions but an instance of a folk classification. The *caldos* we ate in Goias and Minas Gerais were quite thick and served in bowls. This type of soup is particularly common in these two "heartland" states.

Beans, Beans, Beans!

There are numerous variations on bean dishes, and Minas offers several very well-known ones. *Tutu a Mineira* is perhaps the most characteristic and valued Mineiran dish. As a relatively prestigious dish, it is often served with more elaborate cuts of meat such as a whole pork loin or a suckling pig with crispy skin. Alongside these principal ingredients one finds an array of side dishes, including fried pork rind and sautéed greens. *Tutu* is a purée of black beans that is cooked first and then puréed and flavored with bacon fat and onion before being reheated and garnished with a hard-boiled egg. It is the Brazilian equivalent of refried beans and very tasty.

A second very important style is *feijão tropeiro*, which traces its ancestry back to the early explorers and exploiters of the inland region, in which it has become a popular regional dish. These explorers were called *Bandeirantes*, so named for the flag or banner they carried into the hinterland to claim the regions for the Portuguese Crown, and in the process, not incidentally, to find riches for themselves and slaves to work the mines (Burns 1993: 55–57; Eakins 1997: 22; Vianna Moog 1964). Since they were constantly on the move, on foot, horseback, or on mules, they did not carry much luggage with them. This dish included ingredients that were relatively light and easily transported: beans, *farinha*, and dried meat (often beef), which would not spoil when carried across long distances. They only needed to be boiled up, usually together, to make a hearty dish. *Feijão tropeiro* is featured in restaurants and homes as a regional dish.

A third dish of beans, called *baião-de-dois* (literally "dancing in a couple") combines rice with green peas or beans similar to cowpeas, and mixes them with cheese and onion. This dish is particularly associated with the Northeast region of Brazil but is also popular in many other regions. Each of these bean dishes garners loyal fans, for whom the food represents a form of comfort food, familiar, homey, and satisfying.

With the beans done or underway, the cook can prepare rice, often accompanied by a side of pasta and a piece of meat. The whole dish when completed may be sprinkled with manioc flour or *farinha*. A fancier way, and one that is also delicious, entails cooking up some garlic in olive oil and sautéing the *farinha* in the oil until it is lightly toasted. This dish, called *farofa*, may be dressed up with any number of additions: onions, tomatoes, peppers, corn, bits of sausage, or a scrambled egg. Different regions have different *farofa* specialties.

Rice, beans, pasta, *farinha*, and meat in greater or smaller proportions are the basis of the *prato feito* or quick meal served in so many stalls or restaurants. These ingredients also form the components of many fancier meals in which each component is cooked in a more elaborate way, for example, pork roast with *tutu a mineira*, *feijoada*, stroganoff over rice, and so forth.

Vegetables as Comfort Food

In addition to beans, several other foods evoke a sense of comfort and home or hominess. One such food is okra, which in many of the diaspora regions is strongly associated with home cooking among Afro-descended populations. The appeal of okra, however, transcends this heritage in Brazil. It is a popular vegetable across the country. One of the characteristic dishes of Minas is *frango com quiabo*, chicken with okra. Sitting next to a young woman on the plane back to Brazil, I chatted with her about her year in the United States and her excitement about going home. I asked what dish she wanted to eat as a homecoming meal, and she answered, without hesitation, *frango com quiabo*. I got the same answer from a young professor in Curitiba who was nostalgic for her Minas Gerais home. This dish is home cooking par excellence, although it is not a lower-class or devalued meal (as evidenced by the fact that this young woman had the money and education to spend a year in the United States). It is essentially a one-dish meal (although usually served with rice) and contains the mixture of tastes and textures that evoke comfort, childhood, and plentitude.

Frango com quiabo

Ingredients

1 free range chicken
Oil
2 sweet peppers
3 tomatoes
½ lb. of okra
Garlic
Bay leaf
Salt to taste
3 bunches of parsley
1 small onion, diced
Black pepper to taste

Preparation

1. Cut the chicken and season it to taste.
2. Wash and cut the okra.
3. Fry the okra in a separate pan.
4. Put the chicken in a pan with oil and cook until it is golden.

5. Remove the excess fat.
6. Add the pepper, okra, and onion and cook until it boils.
7. Add the parsley, tomatoes, and black pepper.
8. Serve with rice. (*Postais de Minas* n.d.)

Pão de Queijo

Minas has also contributed another beloved product, *pão de queijo*, to the national culinary scene. This product has become so ubiquitous that it does not appear to have a regional origin—until you get to Minas Gerais and see the regional pride they have in it. *Pão de queijo* is a cheese bread made with manioc flour and rolled into small balls about one to one-and-a-half inches in diameter and baked until golden. Served warm with butter or jam, it is a delicious and chewy treat served both for breakfast (*café de manhã*) and as a snack or appetizer. One of the most widespread fast food restaurants throughout the country is called *Pão de Queijo*: branches of it are found in shopping malls, airports, and business districts. They serve these cheese-bread balls in snack bags or make them into mini sandwich rolls. The cheese used in this recipe is the mild cow's milk cheese known as Minas cheese that is sold all over the country. The flour used for this roll is *farinha de mandioca*, manioc flour, also widely available; thus, these cheese-bread rolls can be made everywhere in Brazil. These cheese rolls have also become extremely popular outside of Brazil. *Pão de queijo* mixes are now available in some specialty stores in immigrant communities in the United States and Britain, and also through the Internet. Manioc flour has become an important substitute for wheat flour in the production of gluten-free breads.

Getting through the Day

Brazilians are addicted to coffee in many forms. As noted in the previous section, breakfast is called *café de manhã* or "morning coffee." This first coffee of the day is frequently served in a large cup often with hot milk. This drink is called *café com leite* ("coffee with milk") and is often accompanied by a roll or *pão de queijo* as described above. Subsequent cups of coffee are usually drunk in much smaller cups and with espresso-like strength. These "shots" of coffee are strong and sweet. Brazilians like a lot of sugar or sweetener (*adoçante*) in their coffee. Many people (and offices) make a strong pot of coffee and keep it warm in a thermos so as to have a quick infusion of sweet coffee during the day.

Both coffee and sugar have been important plantation crops in Brazil and are among the biggest exports. Coffee production brought a great deal of wealth into São Paulo State and Southern Minas Gerais. Minas was the state in which the two main agricultural exports, coffee in the south and sugar in north, met. A lot of the upper-class families, especially those in São Paulo City, owe their fortunes to coffee *fazendas* ("plantations"). Many of the restaurants and clubs in the large cities were frequented by those with coffee fortunes. Possession of a coffee *fazenda* was a mark of prestige and status.

Historically, coffee was also a symbol of wealth and prestige in Rio de Janeiro in the early nineteenth century. At that time, wealthy men used to frequent the Largo de Palácio on the waterfront in Rio. This *praça* was a large open area, in which a line of raised, stone throne-like chairs lined the walk. The gentry would come and sit on these chairs and be served small cups of coffee (*cafezinho*) by slaves who made and sold the coffee. French artist Jean Baptiste Debret drew a series of pictures portraying scenes of the lives of the gentry of this time, including one of gentlemen being served coffee in these stone thrones (Holston 1989: 112). Although no one drinks coffee in thrones anymore, it is still easy to get a *cafezinho* on the street, beach, or bus as roving vendors make the rounds with cups and thermos.

The Taste of Comfort

Any discussion of daily life has to include the comfort foods of soft, mushy, creamy purées and porridges, many varieties of which are found in most regional cuisines. It is not too much of a cliché to attribute the love of these foods to their association with childhood and the familiar, comfortable nostalgia they may produce. In different parts of the country these dishes are made from different starches depending on what is local or cheap or what the ethnic heritage of the region values: corn, yam, manioc, tapioca, rice, or even potato, can become the center of a meal. Across the country the ingredient, the name, and even the texture of the dish might vary, but the appeal does not. This type of starchy accompaniment is found not only in homes but also in food stalls or street corners. The type of starch used makes it characteristic of a specific place and the different vernacular terms by which it is called, *mingau* or *canjica* or *munguzá*, also help identify its regional origin. In poorer strata of the population, such dishes formed an important part of the diet. These porridges can be served either sweet or savory depending on the time of day or placement in a meal; they can be eaten for breakfast, supper, or with a sweetener as a dessert.

Another variation on such porridge-like foods is represented by the bread-based or manioc-based foods of Bahia. Discussed in Chapter 2, the popular *bobó de camarões* in Bahia takes the classic *moqueca* recipe and inserts it into a manioc purée. The result is a creamy pudding with the flavors of seafood, coconut milk, and *dendê* oil. Combining the seafood *moqueca* with the puréed manioc extends the number of people this dish can serve while combining substance, flavor, and the comfortable texture of porridge. This dish is particularly popular for weekend family meals.

A second such dish in the Bahian repertoire is *vatapá*. *Vatapá* is a thick pudding made with stale bread soaked in coconut milk and flavored with ground cashews, dried shrimp, and *dendê* oil. The soft, mushy texture produced by this combination of ingredients contrasts with the sharp taste provided by the *dendê*. The combination gives this dish a wide appeal as a local classic. Across the country, substantive dishes like *bobó*, polenta, and *pirão* add comfort to the value of *farta*, "fullness," without sacrificing the distinctive flavors of each region.

Doces ("Sweets") Plain or Fancy

As mentioned above, many Brazilians have a sweet tooth and enjoy a sweet ending to a meal. In addition fruits play an important role in home cooking, and Brazil has a rich array of fruit. They are consumed in a variety of ways, from fresh to distilled. Very sweet desserts are the norm in Brazil, especially in the Central and Northeast regions, which were, after all, the center of world sugar production for centuries. Several factors have contributed to the Brazilian repertoire of desserts. On the one hand, the Catholic Church brought monks and nuns to the New World and set them up in monasteries and convents, which often maintained dairy and poultry herds providing eggs, milk, and cream. The nuns especially brought the cake-making culture of Portugal, which used lots of milk, butter, eggs, and sugar to make cakes, tarts, custards, and so forth. They adapted the local fruits to make jams, tarts, and confits in the manner of their Portuguese heritage.

To this day, a buffet of Mineiran food will contain a broad selection of sweets, syrupy fruits, candied fruits and peels, custards, and little tarts, often filled with custard or jam. The easy availability of sugar made this indulgence more available to a bigger proportion of the population than elsewhere. According to popular history, a collusion between mistress and slave made the production of sweets a somewhat illicit gendered activity. Although many middle- and upper-class women had domestic help to cook and clean for them, one of the main contexts in which they worked alongside their servants was in baking and the making of sweets. There are not many records of recipes from the colonial period, but much of what remains are pastry recipes, and these are frequently noted as family recipes passed down through the female line. In the Northeast, in particular, people say that the custom of selling sweets on the streets stems in part from a collaboration between the mistress of the house and her cook to make sweets (*doces*) of sugar, coconut, and chocolate, which the slave or maid would sell on the streets. The two women would share in the profits and each earned a bit of pocket money. Whether or not this is true, selling sweets on the street, on the beach, and at festivals is an important part of the culinary scene and is the provenance of women. Many of the traditionally attired *Baiana* women who sell *acarajés* on street corners also sell coconut and chocolate sweets.

In addition to making these candies, women produced fruit preserves. One of the interesting fruit concoctions in Brazil is the guava paste and Mineiran cheese combination mentioned above. The guava paste and cheese are eaten together directly from a plate or as a sandwich with bread or crackers so that the sweetness and saltiness intermingle. This combination, often served as a dessert, is fancifully named *Romeo e Julieta* to underscore the attraction of opposites. This dessert is served around the country but seems rooted in the food traditions of Minas, since it instantiates the local production of cheese and fruit preserves.

Another type of dessert is that of the custard or pudding (*pudim*) made with milk—often condensed milk—and eggs or fruit. Flan dishes reminiscent of Spain and Portugal are prevalent, as are mousse desserts similar in style to the classic French mousse. A popular dessert across Latin America is the caramel-like treat called *doce de leite* in Portuguese.

Mousse de Maracujá (Passion Fruit Mousse)

Ingredients

1 bottle of passion fruit juice (unsweetened), about 16 oz.
1 can of condensed milk
1 can of *creme* (otherwise called table cream)

Preparation

1. In a blender mix all three liquids together until foamy.
2. Chill until spongy.

Conclusions

Home cooking holds a special place in many people's hearts, as the restaurant names mentioned above seek to evoke. This familiar affect, however, becomes more evocative as "home" recedes in one's daily life. This happens for two main reasons. Firstly, people are more transitory and many no longer live in the city, region, or town that was home growing up. Secondly, people no longer work as close to home as they did and cannot go home for the midday meal. Food helps to bridge both these gaps by enabling many people to forge connections and associations of home through the foods they eat.

Churrasco a Rodízio and *Feijoada Completa*: The Culinary Production of an Imagined National Community

Home food and regional food are important parts of the production of identity and play salient roles in the creation of Brazilian social and cultural life, but there is one more level that needs to be examined: national cuisine. Is there a national Brazilian cuisine? And if so, what makes it national? Many nations do not have a national cuisine or at least one that is acknowledged by all the different parts of a nation. Anthropologists like Mintz (1996) and Appadurai (1988) have talked about the complexities of such classifications and how some foods get elevated to national status. Brazil may or may not have a national cuisine but it certainly has a national dish. Magazines, guidebooks, restaurants, and many individuals all proclaim *feijoada* as the national dish (especially in the form of *feijoada completa*). To *feijoada*, I would add *churrasco*, Brazilian barbecue that is a delicious food and a popular pastime. If there is a face to Brazilian food outside of Brazil, these two meals would be it.

Churrasco and *Churrascarias*

Churrasco is another rendition of the Brazilian love of substantive and plentiful meals. It is the art of cooking meats over a hot fire, either on a grill or on a spit. This form of cooking is frequently done by men (as is grilling in many of the English-speaking countries around the world such as Britain, Australia, and the United States). Beef is the most commonly grilled meat, but Brazilians are creative and innovative and many other meats find places on the grill. Barbecue is imbued with the *gaucho* culture of the South, as much of the meat tradition comes from this cattle-raising region.

Backyard grilling exemplifies this family form of eating and cooking, but the culture of meat and the significance of the barbecue reach extravagant heights through the medium of the *churrascaria*. The *churrascaria* is a restaurant specializing in grilled meat. There are two main kinds of *churrascaria*. Both have a big fire with spits for roasting meat and a grill for broiling or grilling it. In the first, patrons order meals of steak, chicken, and chops off a menu or in consultation with a waiter. The second form is often called *rodízio*, which means "making the rounds." The main attraction of restaurants *a rodízio* is the big fire over which various cuts of meat are roasted on large spits pointed like swords. When the meat is cooked, the spits are removed from the fire and waiters carry them around the dining room in one hand while brandishing a large knife in the other. The waiter pauses at each table and cuts off slices of meat as indicated by the patron. The form of the meal is all one can eat, and the waiters keep serving until the customer signals that he (or she) can eat no more. Often patrons are provided with a small coaster that has a green symbol on one side signifying a desire for more meat, and a red signal meaning "no more" (at least for the present). Customers may sit and rest between bouts of eating. The meats can vary from the basic cuts of beef, sausages, chicken, and some pork or lamb to chicken hearts, pheasant, the hump of a zebu cow, or wild boar, roast suckling pig, or goat. This style of barbecue is particularly Brazilian, but it has developed in the southern part of the country in the areas closest to the heavy meat and barbecue regions of Argentina and Uruguay.

Many *churrascarias* combine the buffet-style cuisine found in *a quilo* restaurants with the Southern specialization of *churrasco* or "barbecue." *Churrascarias* usually have a buffet of appetizers and side dishes, to which patrons are directed as soon as they sit down. Some side dishes may also be brought to the table: these include French fries, onion rings, fried bananas, fried polenta, and others. The traditional buffet had salads, breads, rice, and accompaniments such as *farofa*. Today's buffets have shrimp, cheeses, sausage, sushi, small pastries (*salgados*) of meat or cheese, multiple salads, eggs, fish, pasta, and so forth. Some even have such luxuries as oysters. They are enormous arrays of food. Many *churrascarias* offer a two-tiered menu: just the buffet, or the buffet plus *rodízio* of meat. Each of these options is a *prix fixe*, one price for as much as you can eat.

Interestingly, what fewer and fewer *churrascarias* have is beans. Beans are not always served in this context, whereas they are served in multiple forms in the *comida a quilo* restaurants. One informant explained this by saying that since beans were eaten at virtually every meal at home, people want to eat something different when they go out. Although this is only one person's analysis, it fits with the idea that the *a quilo* restaurants are a substitute form of home cooking while most other restaurants represent the opposite. Of course, beans are available *a la carte* in *churrascarias* as well.

The difference in offerings is, perhaps, attributable to the different regional origins of these eating styles. The *comida a quilo* owes much to its origins as home cooking from the "heartland," that is, states like Minas Gerais, and emphasizes the foods of that tradition. The *churrascaria* evolved from a Southern style of eating and cooking, heavily influenced by ranchers, and reflects the more recent European origins of many of the residents. The heavy emphasis on meat makes this an elite form of eating in the rest of the country. Nevertheless, most towns have popular *churrascarias* and many smaller eateries, including bus stations and buffets, have *chapas* or grills on which meats and sausages are grilled, often to order (*feita na hora*) and often priced by weight.

Feijoada

The opposition between home cooking and fancier alternatives, between paying by the gram or one price for all you can eat, is played out in yet another context, however, and that is the Saturday *feijoada* meal. As mentioned above, *feijoada* is often touted as the national dish of Brazil. It is a rich stew of beans, a variety of meats, and flavorings. Usually served as a *feijoada completa* ("complete *feijoada*"), the festive meal includes an array of side dishes including rice, sautéed *couve* ("collard greens"), oranges, *farofa*, and an uncooked salsa of onions, tomatoes, peppers, cilantro, and dressing. The mythical origins of this dish attribute it to the culinary skills of the slaves who could make a tasty dish out of the remnants and leftovers from the master's house (Camara Cascudo 1983: 501). As discussed in the previous chapter, it parallels dishes from the Southern American Soul Food repertoire that are attributed to the same ancestry. On the other hand, *feijoada* also bears a strong resemblance to multiple dishes from Europe, such as French cassoulet, Tuscan fava beans or chickpeas cooked with meat, or especially the eponymous *feijoadas* from Portugal (Camara Cascudo 1983: 502–3). This dish thus appeals across a wide spectrum of regional and ethnic groups.

Feijoada works as a national dish not just because it embodies the mixed history and heritage of Brazil but because it creates an imagined community in Anderson's sense of the phrase (1991). *Feijoada* is traditionally served as the midday meal on Saturdays,[1] although many restaurants also serve it on Wednesdays. It is usually consumed by an extended family in a long and leisurely afternoon of eating, visiting, watching a soccer game, more eating, or napping. To accompany the meal adults drink beer, *cachaça* (often mixed with fruit juice to make a *batida*, or *caipirinha*). People often comment on the need to have a siesta (*sesta*) after this meal.

The Brazilian *feijoada* should have several different kinds of meat in it, which in totality draws together specialties of different regions. Nowadays, it should include dried beef or salted meat,[2] smoked meat, tongue, sausage, and pork pieces, including the ears, feet, and tail of a pig (and in the more elite versions, a pork roast). Traditionally it was based on the marginal and cheaper cuts of meat; these include snout, ears, tails, feet, and the various organs of a pig. The symbolism of the pig tail and pig's ear is legend, instantiating the cast-off pieces of meat given to slaves after butchering, and later sold in the poorer parts of town. Although with increasing wealth, the *feijoada* is frequently filled with more elite cuts of meat, many cooks and restaurants honor tradition and include pigs' tails and ears in their casseroles. In different regions of Brazil, the preferred bean varies. In Rio and Minas Gerais *feijoada* is made from black beans; in São Paulo I have had black and red beans; in Goias, and Bahia, the preferred bean is brown or red (*mulatinho*); in the Northeast, the preferred bean is variegated.[3] The kind of bean you use says a lot about where you are from even though most people concede that there is virtually no difference in taste. One family in Goias with whom I spoke has lived there for at least two generations but originally came from Rio. The daughter who has lived her whole life in Goias described how her parents, and now she, always made their *feijoada* with black beans, even though she admitted that the black beans cost more in Goias and tasted the same. When I went to a *feijoada*[4] in Salvador, Bahia, it was announced as a *São Paulo feijoada* because the dish was made with black beans. When I described this event to other Salvadorians they seriously argued among themselves about whether it should be called *feijoada paulista* or *feijoada carioca*[5] since both these regions use black beans and the dish is essentially identical in both regions. The principal bean used in Bahia is reddish brown and is called *mulatto* or *mulatinho* ("little *mulatto*"), a term for mixed-race people.

Preparing *Feijoada*

Making a *feijoada completa* is a multiday project. Since the dish is traditionally served on Saturday, the preparations may begin on Thursday. First, the dried beef must be reconstituted several days prior to the serving: this requires soaking the meat in several changes of cold water for about twenty-four to thirty-six hours. Next, the beans have to be soaked for several hours and are usually cooked at least a day before the final serving. The dried meat is then cooked separately first, and later with the mixture of smoked meats, fresh meats, and sausage. The precooked meat is then added to the beans, which are then cooked together until they have shared their flavors. Finally the beans are flavored with sautéed onions, garlic, green peppers, possibly hot peppers, cilantro, and salt and pepper.

The beans and meat stew constitutes the *feijoada*. The full meal, called *feijoada completa*, consists of the stew served with rice; very finely slivered collard greens sautéed in garlic and oil; slices of orange; a raw salsa made of tomato, onion, pepper, and cilantro; and a *farofa* of manioc flour sautéed with garlic and onion; and often other additions like peppers or egg. Thus this dish requires intensive labor and results in a large volume of food, fitting for an extended family meal. The meal is traditionally served in separate plates or bowls, with the meats removed from the beans and sliced and served on a separate platter, surrounded by plates of greens, and bowls of rice, *farofa*, oranges, and salsa. Because of the number of dishes and the number of people, the food is frequently served buffet-style, and people frequently make several trips back to the food table. The whole event is enjoyed as a large and noisy family gathering. Traditionally, extended families would gather at one home (often that of the matriarch/patriarch) for Saturday *feijoada*, and the large and heavy meal would be eaten midday. The satisfaction that people feel eating this meal was summed up by my host "father" in Salvador, who upon sitting down with his third serving, sighed, "I just love *feijoada*." After such a feast, a nap (preferably in a hammock) or lazy promenade is considered appropriate.

Feijoada

Ingredients

1 lb. of dried meat (available in Latin American markets), can be omitted if unavailable.

1–2 lbs. of smoked meat (ham hocks, smoked turkey wings)

1 smoked beef tongue (if available)

3–4 lbs. of fresh pork (a loin roast works well, or a pork butt)

1 lb. of sausage (Brazilian *linguiça* is traditional, but *choriço* or Italian sausage or a mixture of sausages or even smoked turkey sausage can be substituted)

½ lb. of salt pork or bacon

1–2 pig's ears or pig's tail, or both (can be omitted but is traditional in Brazil)

2 lbs. of dried black beans

1 onion

1–2 green peppers

1–2 tomatoes

1 hot pepper

3–4 cloves of garlic

Cilantro

Preparation

1. If using dried or salted meat, start soaking it two days before and change the water several times.
2. The day before serving, put the beans in a large pot of water and bring it to a boil. When it boils, turn it off and soak the beans for an hour. Drain, add more water, and cook.
3. Add bay leaf and/or parsley to beans.
4. Cook the salt pork or bacon, the sausage, and the smoked meat in a pot of water for 10–15 minutes.
5. When the beans start to soften, add all the meats (they can be in large pieces that will later be served on the side or cut and diced in bite-sized pieces) and cook for 1½ hours, partly covered until the beans are tender but not thoroughly cooked. Add water as necessary and stir occasionally to keep the beans from sticking.
6. Set aside in the refrigerator (or outside in the winter) until the next day.
7. On the serving day, bring the meat and beans to a simmer in the large pot, keeping it all moist.
8. Dice the onion, tomato, peppers, garlic, and cilantro.
9. In a large pan add olive oil, and sauté first the onion, then the garlic, then the peppers, and finally the tomato and cilantro. When the vegetables are cooked, add 3–4 large spoonfuls of beans to the pan and mash them with the onion-pepper-tomato mixture.
10. Stir the vegetable/bean mixture back into the beans and meat to thicken.
11. Heat until done.

12. Serve the beans in a bowl, and you can remove all the meats, slice them, and serve on a platter alongside, or add back to the pot.
13. *Feijoada* is served with white rice, toasted manioc flour (*farofa*), and sautéed greens (collard or chard), slices of orange, and a *molho cru* (raw salsa). The rice is served first, the beans and meat are placed over the rice, and the mound is sprinkled with *farofa* and drizzled with orange slices and orange juice. The salsa and greens are placed on the side.

Couve: Sautéed Greens to Accompany *Feijoada*

Ingredients

1½ or 2 lbs. of collard greens
2 tablespoons of olive oil
1–2 cloves of garlic, sliced or diced
Salt and pepper to taste

Preparation

1. Fold the leaves in half lengthwise and cut out the stem.
2. Roll the leaves like a cigar and cut into thin ribbons.
3. In a large skillet, cook the garlic in the olive oil until golden.
4. Add the collard greens and cook, stirring until wilted and covered in oil.
5. Season to taste.

Molho Cru: Uncooked Salsa to Accompany *Feijoada*

Ingredients

1 red onion, finely chopped
1 small green pepper, cored, seeded, and finely chopped
1 medium tomato, finely chopped
¾ cup of olive oil
½ cup of red or white wine vinegar
Salt and pepper to taste

Preparation

1. Combine the ingredients and mix thoroughly.
2. Cover and refrigerate until ready to use.

Feijoada is both a celebration of the everyday meal of beans and meat and an exaggeration of it. If Brazilians extol *comida farta* or filling food, *feijoada* is its epitome. This food represents the home, the history of the people, and the way food binds people together. Eating *feijoada* on Saturdays in the bosom of one's family means

Figure 6.1 A bounteous display of the *feijoada completa* with multiple meats, beans, greens, and *farhinas* arrayed in separate pots. Photograph by Jane Fajans.

that the family continues to congregate, exchange news, add members through birth and marriage, and mourn the loss of others. Even when families no longer gather for this meal, they eat it to evoke the memories (*saudade*) of those times, and in so doing instill, at least to a degree, those thoughts and memories in their children. The idea that people all over Brazil are sharing in this same meal, at virtually the same time, with some or all of the same emotions, is what makes this the national dish. It is a shared experience that need not be shared on all occasions to become meaningful when eaten or thought about.

Nowadays, some of the infrastructure that enabled this home-produced meal to fulfill these functions has dissipated. Families do not all live in close proximity. Fewer families have live-in maids or cooks to assist in the preparation (and clean up), and other activities have impinged on family time. Restaurants now offer a variety of *feijoada* meals to fill the void created by changing lifestyles. These restaurant options range from take-out or delivery of the whole meal to eat at home and thus mimic the one previously prepared at home, to a restaurant buffet with multiple meats in chafing dishes and a selection of rice, beans, and accompaniments. Some restaurants still serve the *feijoada* in an individualized clay pot served at each table with assorted meats flavoring the beans, thus making an attempt to reproduce the family intimacy of the occasion. Others have adapted the meal to the model of the "all you can eat" buffet. They make a big display of the various ingredients, separating out the many meats into separate chafing dishes, and allowing clients to choose among them and add their own trimmings. These restaurants have also expanded the range of accompaniments and appetizers to match the expanding expectations of the middle class who also frequent the *churrascarias* and other restaurants. This event no longer takes up the whole afternoon (let alone the several days preceding it), although many patrons linger in the restaurant and return multiple times to the buffet, conforming with the all-afternoon ethos of the traditional meal. Both versions, home and restaurant, allow participants to feel satisfied and comforted. *Feijoada* embodies tradition, memory (*saudade*), and comfort. It is everyday food raised to a festive level, but it retains strong connections to its roots.

How did a country with such strong regional cuisines end up with a "national dish," and why is that dish *feijoada*? As I mentioned before, the history of this dish is mythically bound up with the slave history in Brazil, and the dish has come to represent the alchemical transformations that poor people, particularly slaves, create out of meager ingredients (Fry 1977). In this sense the story parallels the narrative about Soul Food in the Southern United States (Hughes 1991; Harris 2011: 89–109), except that Soul Food has not risen to the status of national dish but is rather one variant of a regional Southern cuisine. There are lots of possible explanations for this difference, starting with the difference in slavery. Although prominent in both places, the percentage of the population descending from slaves is much greater in Brazil (more than 50% by some estimates[6]) than in the United States, and mainly for this reason, Brazil remained an agricultural society much longer than the United States and arguably still is. The second major consideration comes from the way that beans and rice and some form of manioc became the foundation of a meal in Brazil (as it did in much of Latin America) but not in the United States.

Rice and beans are known by nutritionists to be a very healthy combination, as described in the previous chapter. The two foods complement each other and provide the complete amino acid sequence necessary for a balanced diet. If the diet then includes even a modicum of meat, it suffices for a basic diet. Beans are usually considered native to the New World (although some species were available in other parts of the world prior to the Colombian Exchange) and certainly the red and black varieties most commonly used in *feijoada* are indigenous (Albala 2007). Rice, although found throughout Asia, was probably brought to the New World from West Africa, and cultivated by slaves and their descendants across the east coasts of the Americas (Carney 2001). Meat and bean dishes exist as important regional dishes throughout Europe and Africa as well as the Americas and Caribbean (e.g., Cajun rice and beans, Boston baked beans). These ingredients thus mimic the major populations of which the Brazilian nation was composed in the nineteenth century. Rice is now grown extensively in much of the Americas and remains an affordable staple. Rice is the key staple throughout much of Asia and parts of the Middle East and Africa and thus appeals to immigrants and their descendants from all those regions as well. In Goias, faculty at the *Centro de Educação Profissional* (a new culinary education program) discussed food patterns and preferences and asserted that Goianos really love rice. They eat lots of rice and mix it with local specialties such as *piqui* and *quiabo*. One professor commented, "A nice pot of fresh rice really pleases." In addition, rice is quite cheap and filling, so it has increasingly become the basic food of the poor in the central part of the country. Manioc, which was a staple for much of the indigenous population, remains an important alternative starch and is frequently served with the rice and beans, most commonly in the form of manioc flour or *farinha*. A dish that combines all these ingredients is one that can please an enormous number of people.

Despite its ubiquitousness, Camara Cascudo, the premier historian of Brazilian food, suggests that *feijoada* in the form of *feijoada completa* did not really exist as a dish until the very end of the nineteenth century (1983: 508–10). All the components of the dish existed as important parts of the cuisine, but only gradually have they become elaborated into the festive and stylized meal they form today. The assertion that *feijoada* is the national dish implicitly entails several claims, none of which are unproblematical. The first is that the dish has resonance and appeal for all nationals. The second is that it transcends regional differences. The third is that it transcends class. The fourth is that it symbolically instantiates the nation. The latter is the claim that may be hardest to substantiate except in the superficial sense of pointing to the multiple origins of the ingredients as symbolically meshing all the components of the population.

I have met a few Brazilians who do not like and do not eat *feijoada*; not many, but a few. I have met quite a few others who do not eat it regularly as a weekly meal. For the most part, however, the dish does seem to have a strong appeal that combines comfort, familiarity, flavor, and the ability to fill one up. I have eaten elite *feijoadas* with plentiful meat and a great variety of ingredients; I have also eaten quite a few in which beans formed the bulk of the stew and meat was in scarce supply, but in which the dish was served up with aplomb. These experiences can be cited in support of the claim that *feijoada* fulfills the criteria of a national dish, at least in the cultural imagination of most Brazilians. Cultural imagination, however, often conceals as well as reveals social aspects of the phenomena at issue. As I discuss in a moment, the myth of *feijoada* as a national dish also mystifies important class relations.

Da Matta has written that there are three cultural events that are truly democratic institutions in Brazil because they override divisions of class (and race). These are carnival, soccer, and the beach (1986; 1991). None of these institutions are actually truly democratic, but they all retain the appearance of equal access and shared participation. Camara Cascudo also describes how visitors to Brazil are unable to understand the essential importance, meaning, and love that the Brazilians have for beans (Camara Cascudo, 1983: 503). He talks about how visitors can appreciate a wide variety of Brazilian foods, but do not register the way that beans surpass these foods in value. Here I have tried to show that beans shine in the local cuisine because they embody so many of the transformations that underlie Brazilian society. Beans can be grown in small family plots or yards. They can be stored for long periods. They combine well with a variety of other foods and flavors, and they are filling, imparting a sense of *farta*. Although foods of the poor, they are enjoyed by the rich and can thus represent the integration of rich and poor, white and black, free and slave, European, African, Japanese, and Native American. On these grounds, one might well nominate the *feijoada completa* for inclusion in Da Matta's list.

The history of the classic *feijoada* parallels the narrative of Brazil as a mixture of indigenous, European, and African ancestry and the story told about *feijoada* reflects those associations in a culinary sense. The pot of *feijoada* is indeed a melting pot. This historical perspective differs from that in the United States, which shares this confluence of ethnic groups, because Brazilian *feijoada* equalizes the three components. In America, the Afro-American cuisine is classified as a regional cuisine and has not had the same success transcending its regionalism to become a national symbol. In Brazil, the myth of the poor and enslaved using their skills to raise a plain and homey dish to the heights of a gastronomic treat functions as an allegory for Brazil's national struggle. This unity is further enhanced by the assumption that *feijoada* is eaten by "everyone" at the same time on the same day, thus allowing everyone to embody and share this essence and identity.

The irony of this whole scenario, however, replays the contradictions of Brazil's history. It is the middle and upper classes who enact this scene of national unity. Backstage one finds the lower classes cooking, serving, and cleaning up so their patrons can consume and digest in a leisurely fashion. Despite the myth that *feijoada* is a national dish, a whole sector of the country does not partake in the ritual except as laborers. If they do eat *feijoada*, they eat it as leftovers in the kitchen or in packages they are allowed to take home. They are not included as "family" or granted commensal relations through eating together.

Because of this national repast, maids in Brazil traditionally have to work on Saturdays just to make this family reunion possible. Not only does the housekeeper/cook have to work, but she often has to enlist the help of a sister or daughter to accompany her and help out with this extra-large meal. Although domestic workers usually have Sundays off, they are frequently expected to accompany "their families" on weekend or week-long excursions. These trips require that they leave their own families to fend for themselves, often in single-parent households to begin with (Goldstein 2002) or bring some or all of them along to enjoy the "country." On one occasion when I was taken on a weekend outing, the *empregada*, her husband, and two young children were all toted along. The woman cooked and cleaned while her husband did odd chores around the country house and yard, but the two young boys were free to play in the pool and run around the yard. Both families saw this as compensation for the additional labor and travel.[7]

The imagined community of everyone eating the same food at the same time, however, fails to address these inequities of class, and of course, of race, since the majority of such domestic workers are black. In being transformed from a modest stew into a celebratory meal, *feijoada* comes to instantiate the inequalities of race and class, of rural and urban communities, and the values of work and leisure. Those who work to prepare this meal rarely get to enjoy it in the way others imagine it. Those who eat to repletion and are so full that they can do nothing for the rest of the day resist thinking about those who work to make this event possible. This, rather than the myths of equal participation, democracy, and transcendence of class, is actually the sense in which the *feijoada completa*, its preparation, performance, and social inequity, at once legitimized and misrepresented by its myths of origin and community, does become a social and symbolic microcosm of the nation and a model for its imaginary national consciousness.

The contradictions of these race and class relations become obscured, however, when Brazilians move away from Brazil. Expatriate Brazilians extol *feijoada* as the instantiation of home and a source of pride in their identity. Introducing foreign friends and neighbors to the national dish becomes a way of describing and sharing the essence of being Brazilian. The meal simultaneously incorporates the foundation of rice and beans, the value of *farta*, and the desire for a large and extended community of eaters. These emotions are all expressed when putting on a *feijoada completa* in a foreign land. The irony of the performance, however, lies in the fact that most Brazilians living abroad cannot afford the sort of domestic help that makes these events possible in Brazil. Families living overseas have to learn new ways of maintaining a household that includes shopping and cooking for itself. Nonetheless, the nostalgia for *feijoada* overrides the work involved and families pitch in to re-create a bit of home through food and company. In this sense *feijoada* becomes, perhaps, an even more inclusive dish that transcends regions and nations, classes, genders, and races. Those who seek to enjoy *feijoada* overseas also learn to make it and thus make themselves in the act of this production.

−7−

The Chemistry of Identity:
Cooking up a New View of a Nation

Global interest in food, gastronomy, tourism, and distinction has spawned a growing industry in restaurants, cookbooks, magazines, culinary tours, and food imports and exports. One of the most interesting trends is the emergence of premier and celebrity chefs who can ignite fascination with new ingredients and fusion cuisines. A growing cadre of premier chefs in Brazilian cities is using and experimenting with the ingredients and even the techniques of the outlying parts of the country. Inspired by fusion cuisine, these chefs are also creating an integration and exchange of food and value that reflects the geography and cultures of the nation.

Over the last five to ten years these chefs and restaurants have become increasingly prolific and popular. They are also producing not just food, but food writings in the form of both cookbooks and theoretical works. A new national cuisine is being created through these productions. They are also garnering international attention as they travel, lecture, and demonstrate in cities around the world while their restaurants win stars and awards. These new celebrity chefs play on the meanings that foods and ingredients have in situ but are not bound by the same strictures that constrain these comestibles in their places of origin. On the whole their experiments have been successful, but in some cases they raise the ire of more traditional preparers and consumers of dishes or ingredients who are invested in the originals. This raises questions about the intended audience for this cuisine. For whom are these foods, dishes, and menus prepared? How important is it that a consumer recognizes the food as innovative or fusion rather than just good food? Does this class of patrons gain distinction not just from the consumption and enjoyment of fine dining, but because there is an extra level of status acquired through understanding the elements of a meal separately and in their combined form?

The New Restaurant Cuisine

Recently, a number of restaurants have opened in Brazil that promote and extol the diversity of Brazilian food. These restaurants themselves illustrate the range and diversity of people's perceptions, values, and interests in different foods. I have already referred to a few such venues. In Pará, one of the best-known restaurants is *Lá en Casa*, owned and run by Paulo Martins. Martins has evolved from local chef to regional food expert and has recently been touted as an ecological chef. He has bridged the gap between regional and cosmopolitan, and his two restaurants are popular with both local residents and tourists. His original restaurant lies in the old sector of town near the *Praça do Republica*. Tourists and locals frequent the restaurant, and Martins is often seen fraternizing with friends and clients. His second restaurant is located among a group of upscale restaurants in the renovated warehouses of the Belém riverside *docas* ("docks"). This modern complex was described to me with pride by a taxi driver as "*muito Primeiro Mundo*" ("very First World"). These renovated warehouses are located along the Amazon River bank just a few feet along from the *Ver-o-Peso* market described in Chapter 3. Despite this proximity, the two venues cater to very different clientele. As one market vendor explained, he had never been to the *docas* because it was not for the poor, it was for the rich (Leitão 2010: 90). The restaurant chefs frequent the market next door, but the market vendors do not penetrate the clean and air-conditioned restaurants and bars inside. These restaurants are frequented by both tourists and young affluent locals.

Martins has promoted Paraense food around Brazil and abroad in venues such as *Terra Madre* events. He is called upon as a spokesperson for the region. He has made a DVD and cookbook combination as a pilot for a national series on regional cuisine (2005). He creates regional recipes using local ingredients while also satisfying the Brazilian desire for *comida farta*. His restaurant has a very popular buffet (*prix fixe*) for lunch and weekends. His establishments offer a range of local favorites from *pato no tucupi* to *maniçoba* and *vatapá*. He also provides a tasting menu of a range of locally available fish with regional sauces. His dishes use ingredients seen as local such as *açaí* in such nonlocal items as cakes and puddings. Moreover, he adheres to the local beliefs about foods like *açaí*, especially the idea that it makes a person drowsy and heavy and should only be eaten when a nap is possible. Overall, he promotes the idea that food should be locally sourced and sustainably acquired.

While extolling local recipes, Martins does not adhere to them dogmatically. He also pursues the goal of making the classic dishes of the region a bit more cosmopolitan. On the restaurant menu he offers a section called *creatividade*, which showcases his adaptations of traditional foods such as *tacacaxique*, "chic *tacacá*," with more refined ingredients, more seafood, and a milder *tucupi*. Other embellished dishes include a fish steak with a creamy *bacuri* sauce and a crab claw Milanese.

Martins talks about the global search for new ingredients that he sees as a large component of contemporary cuisine. He suggests that the most promising places to search for such new foods are China and the Amazon. Since China is essentially closed, in his view, to such exploration, that leaves the Amazon. He feels he is positioned to help explore the frontier of these new foods and their uses. In this mode, he positions himself in the same vanguard as Alex Atala.

This new restaurant cuisine coincides with the growing movement to collect and publish recipes in cookbooks. The Paraense/Amazonian cookbooks are all quite recent. The cookbooks for Pará are part of a national and global trend to publish regional cookbooks showing the specialties of each region. SENAC[1] has been producing lavishly illustrated books of this sort for the last ten years. Well-documented and beautifully illustrated, these books are oriented beyond the local market to those who do not socially and culturally embody the recipes and background necessary to produce this cuisine. In particular the SENAC series appears to be designed for a tourist market since, in addition to lavish photos, the books have either English or Spanish translations to appeal to a wider audience. Although there are almost a dozen such SENAC regional collections, each is primarily sold in its respective region of origin. For example, I have not seen Pará cookbooks for sale in Bahia or São Paulo, or Bahian books in Rio, and I have looked. The fact that these books can only be acquired in the region they cover means that possession of such a book becomes a token identifying the buyer as someone who has been to the region in question, and by implication, eaten that region's authentic food. The owner thus gains an element of distinction in the gastronomic world.

Ofir Oliveira appears to offer the same approach to local, regional, and ecological food values as Martins, but as a social activist, he works to give foods (and the values with which they are imbued) a pronounced political meaning. He buys local or raises the food himself and cooks the food in traditional ways. Despite the fact that he was a chef in a Parisian restaurant for ten years, since his return Oliveira describes himself as a community leader who cooks and teaches in the context of an NGO, *Sabor Selvagem*, which seeks to preserve the environment and the way of life of the people who live in it. In addition, he travels widely to disseminate information about his movement. A participant in *Terra Madre* and Slow Food conferences, he lectures about food and its relation to the environment.

Both of these Paraense chefs root their cuisine in the local cultural ecology, but Oliveira appears to be more "hands on" in producing the ingredients as well as the dishes. Both men lecture and travel, as ambassadors of their region, to promote the local food and drink. Oliveira has also appeared on the travel show *No Reservations* with Anthony Bourdain.

I contacted Oliveira after seeing Bourdain's show. His restaurant, which is in his home, was closed for renovations, but he agreed to prepare a dinner for a small group of anthropologists in Belém for a conference. In the course of our dinner, Oliveira elaborated not only on the dishes he prepared and the provenance of the ingredients but also on the culture of the region and the changes it is undergoing. The dishes he chose to cook were focused on highlighting particular ingredients and their local importance. The values of these goods and ingredients derived from their connections to different parts of the region's history. His food hove closely to local recipes but ranged beyond what was readily available in restaurants in the town because he sought and used a wider range of regional ingredients. He also had an aesthetic sense of flavor and proportion, so although the dishes were derived from traditional recipes, they were made with a chef's-eye sensibility. Most of the ingredients were of indigenous origin: tapioca, *farinha*, *jambú*, *tucupí*, heart of palm, wild rice (of a different origin than that of the North American indigenous communities[2]), *bacurí*, *piquí*, Brazil nuts, and various Amazon freshwater fish species such as *arubé* and *piracui* (Oliveira 2011).

Several of Oliveira's dishes had a more European or African flavor, using coconut milk, ginger, and chicory; many of these dishes were baked in earthenware casserole dishes or cauldrons, thus combining European and indigenous methods of cooking. Oliveira also described the African influence on Amazonian cuisine, which he attributed to the influx of slaves from the Northeast of Brazil during colonial times. The connections of this cuisine with the migrations of this population from Africa to Brazil, and then within Brazil, are evident both in history and flavor, but in the Amazon region, these dishes are not seen as introduced. Rather, residents view them as being embedded in the locality. Other local chefs have also claimed dishes such as *vatapá* and *caruru* as regional specialties (Carioca 2008). In fact, as we have seen, these dishes have taken on local identities and have lost much of their African content, particularly because of the absence of *dendê* oil in the dishes.

One of the major differences between markets in Pará and the Northeast (including Bahia) is the distribution of *dendê* oil and *tucupí*. Northeastern markets are filled with plastic bottles of *dendê* oil. These bottles are unlabeled and reused; many are recycled from other oils or soft drink beverages. The vendors are often the same people who make and bottle the oil. The same recycled and unlabeled bottles appear in the markets of Pará and across the Amazon region, but here they are filled with an individual producer's brand of *tucupí*. These bottles are sold as "*tucupí de José*" or "*tucupí de Rosa*." The local qualities of the condiment are reflected in the local production and marketing, and the idiosyncratic use of herbs and spices selected by the maker. Different housewives and chefs have preferred vendors. These market products epitomize the local flavor of the food. *Dendê* is not sold in Pará, just as *tucupí* is not marketed in the Northeast, but the home-bottled presentation of the products is common to both regions.

Rescuing Traditional Cuisines

Another movement around regional food comes from local historians, chefs, and community members who are undertaking what they call "rescue" (*resgata*) operations on regional cuisines. Chef Oliveira is an advocate of the *resgata* movement, in his case for preserving the Paraense cuisine. A different example of a "rescue" operation on a regional cuisine is the revitalization of *fazenda* ("plantation") cuisine in the Central Western state of Goias. The doyenne of this effort is Thelma Pereira Lopes, the owner of the Casa Babilônia outside the resort city of Pirenópolis, Goias. Casa

Babilônia was a sugar plantation and refinery founded in the eighteenth century. The Lopes family acquired it in 1864 when it was still a plantation using slave labor (slavery was not abolished until 1888). Nowadays, it is essentially a museum showcasing the *engenho* ("sugar crusher") and large vats for boiling and crystallizing the sugar, as well as the farm equipment for ranching and cattle raising that followed the demise of the sugar operations, the quarters for farm hands (post–slave labor), and the heart of the *fazenda*, the farmhouse kitchen. In this kitchen she serves a weekend midday meal.

Dona Thelma has researched and recreated a farm menu of extensive proportions and serves up to twenty items each weekend as a brunch or midday meal. The large, semiopen kitchen-dining room has long trestle tables, benches, and rustic tablecloths. Brunch, in this venue, is cooked on traditional brick and cast-iron griddles with built-in brick ovens. Cooks dressed in nineteenth-century farm attire bring the week's offerings to your table. The food is arrayed on platters, in baskets, and in bowls. The dishes range from fresh seasoned ricotta or Minas-style cheese, to meatballs, sausage, and dried beef (*charque*) sautéed with *farinha*. Baked goods include wheat bread, cornbread, manioc bread, cheese bread, manioc and coconut bread, slave house cake (made with corn, sugar, eggs, cloves, and sugar cane juice), pumpkin cake, *pamonha* (steamed cornmeal mush), molasses, and fruit juices. Dona Thelma makes the rounds of the guests and describes the dishes and the research she has done to revitalize this tradition. She has also researched manioc and contributed to a large volume called *Mandioca: Pão de Brasil* (*Cassava: Bread of Brazil*, 2005). She reminiscences about growing up in a household where *farinha* was the unmarked flour used for making bread, and wheat flour was a special occasion food especially appreciated by her father, who came from the South of Brazil and had grown up with European-style breads. Despite her father's Southern roots, Dona Thelma's own affiliation is with the *cerrado*, the open savannah of the central region of Brazil, which is very fertile and extends for hundreds of miles, reaching to the edges of the Amazon forest (Lopes 2009). This region has local specialties such as *piquí* (*Caryocar brasiliense*), *barú* nuts (*Dipterys alata Vox*), and *jabuticaba* (*Myrciaria cauliflora*) (a fruit often made into a jam).[3]

Regional Ingredients Go National

While Martins and Oliveira promote the regional cuisine of the Amazon from within the Amazon area (with forays to demonstrate and speak outside their region), and Dona Thelma touts the cuisine of Goias from within the state, several chefs from the cosmopolitan center have begun to adopt the ingredients and to some degree the recipes of the regional hinterlands of Brazil. These chefs, centered primarily in Rio de Janeiro and São Paulo (but found in other major metropolitan areas as well), are excited by the flavors and textures available outside the traditional culinary repertoire in which they were trained. Their explorations are inspired in part by the transformative innovations of the Asian fusion scene several decades ago. This style of invention and innovation has spread in recent years and has expanded the gastronomes' repertoire.

Until recently fine dining in Brazil referred to European-style dining, particularly French and Italian cuisines and ambiance. This association shifted with the increased appeal of Asian food, particularly Japanese, and the introduction of fusion cuisine. Restaurant connoisseurship expanded in the 1980s and 1990s. It has taken another couple of decades for the movement to incorporate purely Brazilian innovations, but these transformations have revolutionized the food scene across the country.

Within this more recent movement, however, are at least two distinct trends. In the first trend, chefs aim to preserve the traditional form of a regional dish but to augment its taste, quality, and presentation through methods including, but not limited to, using better cuts of meat, enhancing flavor through the use of seasonings, balancing the flavors and ingredients, and selecting only the freshest and best-quality ingredients. In the second trend, ingredients and some of the techniques used to prepare regional cuisine are taken out of their traditional contexts and incorporated into dishes modeled after French and Italian classical haute cuisine.

Ana Luisa Trajano represents the former type of chef, who has gained great renown in the culinary community of São Paulo. Her restaurant, *Brasil a Gosto* ("The Taste of Brazil"), celebrates her journeys around Brazil, eating, talking, and discussing food and culture in each of her destinations. Her photographic account of these expeditions is published in a book bearing the same name as her restaurant. The restaurant possesses a casual elegance. Simple furnishings in an open plan, glass and brick walls with views onto small gardens, sparse décor of regional folkloric materials, all complement a menu of dishes inspired by the regional cuisines of the Northeast, Amazonian, and Central and Southwestern regions. Trajano talks openly about her appreciation of the cuisines of her parental families' home regions, Céara and Minas Gerais in particular, but she incorporates dishes from her travels too. Her dishes are classifiable as *comida farta* and *comida caseira*; she serves full helpings replete with side accompaniments as opposed to skimpy tasting portions. However, her dishes are artfully arranged and creatively adapted to a gastronomic sensibility. She produces adaptations of *moqueca*, crab cakes, fish dishes, beans, grilled cheese, and crab claws. Her dishes range from fish with *acarajé* dumplings and *vatapá* dressing, to *carne do sol* with beans and manioc, to steak with cowpeas and rice. The desserts are elegant variations of the classic sweets like *brigadeiro* (chocolate fudge-like balls with chocolate sprinkles) to fried bananas with wafers made out of Brazil nuts. She is constantly expanding and announces explorations into new regional cuisines as monthly or seasonal specials.

Trajano talked about her nostalgia for the food of the Northeast when she first arrived in São Paulo. She described how she liked to visit the small *Nordestino* restaurants to eat *paçoca* and *carne do sol* and to absorb the atmosphere of the community that gathered there. Her food reflects her connection to Northeastern cuisine but gives it a more cosmopolitan air. Her nostalgia for the food and scents of home are part of the experience shared by many migrants. She uses her emotional connection to the cuisines to inspire her adaptations (Trajano 2007).

Until recently, many if not most of the Amazonian ingredients that embody the region's distinctive identity and unique flavors were available only within the region. Difficulties of preserving and transporting such ingredients combined with the lack of a market for them kept this cuisine localized. Despite a kind of fetishism surrounding the difficulties of obtaining the ingredients unique to Amazonian cuisine, or perhaps because of it, many of the foods and flavors once confined to this region have been "discovered" by creative chefs in Brazil and used in a new repertoire of dishes. This nouvelle explosion has received a great deal of media attention and has spawned a new set of menus and cookbooks. The centers for these chefs are Rio and São Paulo, but other regions also have restaurants that meld the classic recipes with new culinary sensibilities and add new ingredients to familiar dishes.

Alex Atala is a major leader of this culinary (r)evolution. His signature restaurant, D.O.M., in São Paulo, has been named one of the top restaurants in the world. The interior conveys the atmosphere of a fine dining establishment.[4] The subdued tones, white tablecloths, and formal serving staff reinforce this ambiance. Recently, however, the restaurant has been renovated to open the kitchen to the dining area and bar. Diners are invited to gaze into the kitchen and, at least visually, engage the preparation of their meals; the indigenous artifacts evenly distributed across both areas mark these domains as a single continuous space. Here, Atala experiments with the subtle introduction of more exotic ingredients such as *tucupí* and *jambú*, *dendê* oil, *pimento de cheiro de Pará* (a small round and hot yellow pepper), and Amazonian fish. As one of the premier chefs in Brazil, Atala has been invited to events around the world, including Alimentaria, Madrid Fusion, Salone del Gusto, Slow Food, and Omnivore (Atala 2012). He presents his vision of a Brazilian Gastronomy.

The menu at D.O.M. combines classic fare with surprising tastes and textures. Many of the dishes are small tasting plates, and combine two or three ingredients into a semblance of another dish. He mixes ingredients from classical haute cuisine with these more exotic foods in ways that evoke both traditions. He employs relatively unknown ingredients, often to mimic those better known: for example, he uses manioc to make gnocchi, shredded heart of palm to serve as pasta, and delicate riffs on bean broth with salted cod and sautéed greens. Atala has discovered flavors and spices such as *tucupí*, *jambú*, and *priprioca* (*Cyperus articulatus L*).[5] His multiple-course tasting menu includes combinations such as tapioca and salmon eggs with deep fried oysters; *filhote* (an Amazonian fish) with a crust of *farofa*, a *jambú* flower, and a sauce of *tucupí*; pasta of *palmeira* (shredded heart of palm) served with seared tuna; a *palmito* purée with *castanha de Pará* (Brazil nuts), *jabuticaba* (a fruit from the central *cerrado* of Brazil), and a wasabi sauce; mashed potatoes with *queijo Minas* (cheese from Minas Gerais); and *fois gras* with a sorbet of *cambusi* (a fruit of the *Mata Atlantica*). This same fusion technique can be seen in the cooking of Claude Troisgrois, who has restaurants in New York and Rio de Janeiro and also uses indigenous ingredients in creative and novel ways, such as tapioca pearl caviar, *vatapá* pizza, and *pão de queijo francês*. *Pão de queijo francês* is a French version of the famous Brazilian cheese bread. It is made with wheat flour instead of manioc flour and Gruyère instead of Queijo Minas (Troisgros 2007: 15).

These chefs and many more are transforming both classical haute cuisine and traditional Brazilian cooking. By reaching into the regional cuisines of the country and taking hold of the interesting and creative aspects of very different culinary styles, they are constructing a unique set of ingredients and a varied set of techniques for processing them. This new gastronomic collection is the basis of a uniquely Brazilian cuisine that transcends the regional level and encompasses the separate parts of the nation. In this process we can watch a national cuisine evolving.

Chefs like Atala and Trajano go beyond the superficial or touristic encounter with the Amazon, however. They have become committed to engaging with the people and economy of the regions that they find inspiring. Several years ago, when Atala became enamored with Amazonian ingredients as well as specialties from other areas such as the *Mata Atlantica*, he bought a *fazenda* (farm or ranch) in the state of Amapa, on the north side of the Amazon River. Here, he produces many of the ingredients he uses in the restaurant. He grows and acquires these local ingredients in Amapa and regularly flies them down to his São Paulo restaurant, marketing them as fresh and authentic Amazonian foodstuffs. He hopes to encourage others to grow these ingredients too, and thus to help provide a market for them in the rest of Brazil and internationally. Atala has become something of a proselytizer for the bounty of the country.

Atala, however, has branched out and opened a second restaurant in São Paulo, *Dalva e Dito*, in which he prepares classic Brazilian dishes, or, more accurately, *comida caseira* that is impeccably produced and raised from the ordinary to the extraordinary. He describes this cuisine as paying homage to mothers and grandmothers (*Dalva e Dito* 2011). Through an enormous glass wall, diners in this establishment have an open view of the kitchen and can even seat themselves along the bar facing and in full view of the kitchen as if they were in their mother's or grandmother's kitchen. The restaurant's décor is all brick and heavy wood, but it nevertheless remains light and open because of the high ceilings. One reviewer who enjoyed the food made the wry comment, however, that lunch or dinner at *Dalva e Dito* was a high price to pay for the *prato feito* (see Chapter 5) (Kugel 2009), since the foods tend to mostly comprise rice, beans, meat, and manioc.

Reinventing Indigenous Cuisine

The exploration of Brazil's culinary history has effected a revaluation of both products and the people who make and use them. In particular indigenous cultures have undergone a renewed valuation. A restaurant in Brasília called *Oca dos Tribos* plays upon the aesthetic of the Amazonian indigenous tribes as a backdrop for the fusion cuisines of the world. The setting is lovely, a reproduction of a *maloca* (communal house), made of posts and thatch built in a circle and enclosed on the outside but open to an interior circular plaza in the center. The décor is heavily Amazonian; the space is filled with masks, baskets, and feather headdresses lining the walls and rough-hewn furniture and stools painted in indigenous patterns. The floor alternates stone and tile in a pattern reminiscent of Xinguano mask designs. The food, however, is fusion and has a prominent international, and especially Asian, flavor palate. But Brazilian foods can also be found in abundance. A variety of rice and manioc starches, fish and shellfish entrees, and a grill with meats and sausages as well as pineapples and bananas round out the menu.[6] Situated in the capital of Brazil, home to many embassies and international organizations, this restaurant not only has a global feel but also a global clientele. In my two visits to the restaurant, I was struck by the number of languages spoken at the various tables and the obvious international patronage. There were Africans, Asians, Americans, Europeans, and Brazilians speaking different languages and wearing clothes from different cultures. In order to appeal to a more cosmopolitan audience, the restaurateurs responsible for the *Oca dos Tribos* have attempted to promote the exotic diversity of their own cuisine. In my field notes, I mused that the intention seemed to be to "show the exotic foreigners the 'authentic exotic' of traditional, 'natural' Brazil." The result, however, owes more to a conventional Brazilian notion of the exotic than to authentic indigenous cuisines or

Figure 7.1 Interior of *Oca dos Tribos* restaurant, Brasilia. Photograph by Jane Fajans.

"natural" Amazonian ingredients. In the past, the goal was to rival the grand culinary traditions of Europe and Asia, but now the game has changed. Restaurateurs want to promote the best new thing in global cuisine, and sometimes that best new thing is in their own backyard.

This food movement is self-conscious. Brazilian chefs and connoisseurs are swiftly realizing and seizing upon the bounty of their own country. A movement of this sort, appropriating the regional cuisines of France, Italy, China, or Mexico, is not new, but here is the difference: the new trends seek not only to "rescue" and reproduce the simple cuisines of the hinterlands or indigenous peoples; instead these cuisines and their ingredients are now seen as invaluable contributions to an experimental project of re-creating the gastronomy of the national culture, thus to become integrated into an emergent global cuisine. Many of the participants in this new culinary consciousness are aware of its convergence with culinary patterns in neighboring countries like Argentina, Peru, Colombia, and Mexico, to name some of the obvious comparisons. They meet at conferences, lecture tours, and events like *Terra Madre*, which gives them a sense of community and shared mission. All of the Latin American countries are experiencing this trend toward innovative incorporation of regional recipes and products, but because of its size and wealth, and in part because of its huge diversity in cuisines, ethnic traditions, and climates, Brazilian gastronomy, in particular, is booming.

It is not just chefs who are propelling the new gastronomic wave in Brazil and Latin America. Wealthy and middle-class patrons are becoming intensely interested in sophisticated and innovative cuisine. This clientele follows the trends and openings of restaurants with enthusiasm, both because they enjoy eating and socializing in such venues, but also because they acquire a patina of distinction and sophistication from being a part of this community. These restaurants cater to an educated and cosmopolitan community in the big urban areas and together they build a new Brazilian identity around a creative national cuisine.

From the Table to the Book

Alex Atala has both a creative and an intellectual attitude toward cooking. He proudly showed my husband and me a book he had written (and self-published, I believe) that discusses the structural theories of Claude Levi-Strauss in relation to his own theory of cooking and cuisine (Atala 2007). He starts with Levi-Strauss's culinary triangle and works outward to a new set of diagrams that places various foods along several continuums from raw to cooked and burnt to rotten (Atala 2007). He is particularly interested in the ways these foods gain new flavors as they are processed differently. He classifies flavors as static or dynamic. Overcooked foods are static while dynamic foods are closer to the uncooked or *al dente* phase of preparation. In his taxonomy, the chef is the one who can mix ingredients together in a creative way to add dynamism to static ingredients and life to new dishes. His perspective uses distinctions between raw and cooked, mild and flavored, static and dynamic, to create new and enticing combinations. Interestingly, his take on the ways that foods take on different flavors as they are differently processed is evocative of the multiple products from the single manioc plant described in Chapter 3, although he does not specifically acknowledge this.

In addition to this relatively unknown book, Atala has written or coauthored several others, each of which engages the relations between the raw foodstuffs and the transformative properties of the culinary arts. One is a cookbook in two volumes, *Por uma Gastronomia Brasileira* (*For a Brazilian Gastronomy* 2003), which is a reflection on his own culinary explorations. Another book, co-written with Carlos Alberto Dória, is called *Com Unhas, Dentes e Cuca* (*With Nails, Teeth, and Head* 2008), which examines the relations of raw and cooked tastes and textures, as the groundwork for a creative gastronomy. Atala and Dória are part of a movement within a movement that dialectically synthesizes theory and practice in an attempt to systematize the imagination of a new gastronomy.

Cookbook Culture

Cookbooks have been a growth industry for several decades now, and they have become more and more elaborate and artistic. What used to be a printed collection of recipes with the occasional line drawing of a vegetable, bowl, or implement either in the margins or dividing recipes has morphed into a stunning visual exploration of dishes, cultures, history, and artisanal accompaniments, all lavishly illustrated by beautiful photographs. The first black-and-white Bahian cookbooks I found in 1982 have been superseded by a new set of books I add to every time I visit Brazil. The luscious photos of dishes and ingredients represent a new form of sensual pleasure that Alexander Cockburn has provocatively termed *gastro-porn* (1977). Cookbooks have become coffee-table books equally at home in the living room as in the kitchen. The travelogue of Ana Luisa Trajano, *Brasil a Gosto*, exemplifies this transferability, as it has neither text nor recipes, but is replete with gorgeous pictures of markets, dishes, and local people. Other cookbooks offer a more balanced collection of recipes, instructions, and photos to inspire the reader.[7] In Brazil, as in the United States and United Kingdom, these glossy books are often thematic, ranging from regional to ethnic and from ingredient-oriented to restaurant-inspired. Many have lengthy texts describing the evolution of a gastronomic style or the history of a region.

Several aspects make these new works indicative of the changing culinary scene in Brazil. The first is that until recently in middle- and upper-class families (the target audience for many of these books), the food preparers and food consumers were not the same people. Most households in these classes had maids who also cooked or domestics specially employed as cooks. These domestic workers cooked the food they learned while growing up, or used recipes passed down through apprenticeship in different households. Because domestic workers were frequently poorly educated and, in extreme cases, illiterate, following a recipe from a book was not an option. Although many households still rely on such labor for day-to-day meals, there is a growing interest in cooking and entertaining among young professionals. These are the people who flock to the many fine dining establishments but who are now becoming interested in creating such food at home. They are the intended consumers of these books.

Along with the purchase of such elegant cookbooks, these same consumers are beginning to alter the space in which food is prepared. In the past, and also in many homes at present, most Brazilian houses and apartments were divided into the social and the service sectors (Caldeira 1996; Gillam n.d.; Goldstein 2002; Caldwell 2007; Da Matta and Hess 1995). Maids, cooks, and other service providers had their own entrances, including separate elevators in apartment buildings. The maids' quarters and laundry and kitchen areas were usually in the back and closed off, by several doors, from the social rooms, which the family and their guests inhabited. The new trends in both construction and renovation are making noteworthy strides, whether consciously or unconsciously, in dismantling this segregated pattern. Servant quarters are still distinctly separate from social milieus, but many kitchens are now being remodeled and opened into the social areas so that cooks and guests can visit while a meal is prepared. This change reflects the shift in the household division of labor. Analogous changes can be seen in the design of the trendier new restaurants, such as those of Alex Atala in São Paulo. Although the middle and upper classes still have help who cook and clean for them, fewer have live-in help than they did twenty years ago. Evenings and weekends (or at least after the midday meal on Saturday) are times when the household provides for itself and may entertain others relying on its own resources. Among the many lifestyle magazines in Brazil are sizeable selections focusing on kitchen and bath designs and on cooking and entertaining.

The clientele for all the new cookbooks is not just the newly gourmandized middle class, however. Many of the glossiest cookbooks on Brazilian and regional cuisine are bilingual. These books have sections at the end that translate the text and recipes into either English or Spanish. These works are geared not just to an emerging local interest in food and gastronomy and the reproducibility of both, but are directed beyond the local to the global tourist market as well.[8] This corresponds to the rise in global gastro-tourism and travel that includes an emphasis on dining. Tourists are also a major clientele for the new gastronomic scene. Eating in fine restaurants and exploring new cuisines are a pathway to creating prestige and distinction among educated people. Carrying a cookbook back from such engagements becomes a token of this experience and allows one to both flaunt and re-create one's global experience at the kitchen (or dining) table at home.

From Moonshine to the Cocktail Lounge

Another product that has gone from identification with the poor and regional to high-end and refined is *cachaça*, the distilled alcoholic beverage made from sugar cane.

As we have seen with other aspects of Brazilian food, the value of the food is, at least in part, due to the history and myth that accompany it. This is also true of *cachaça*. Sugar cane was introduced to Brazil in 1532 as the then Portuguese colony's main economic industry. Production of sugar cane in the New World sought to free Europe from expensive and limited supplies of sugar provisioned from the Far East. Sugar was one of the first plantation crops, heralding an industrial agriculture based on a system of monoculture. It depended on a dedicated labor force to cultivate and process the cane. The Portuguese depended on forced labor. They first enslaved local labor, that is, the indigenous population, but when this supply was insufficient due to both increased production and the decimation of Native populations as a result of disease and poor treatment, they turned to importing African slaves from across the Atlantic. Slavery began early in Brazil beginning in 1539. Over the course of two centuries the country received almost 4 million slaves (Masciola 2006). Arguably, sugar molded Brazilian identity; Father Antonio Vieira[9] even equated the product with the country in statements such as, "Brazil was sugar and sugar was the black man" (quoted in Masciola 2007).

In addition to making refined sugar from the sugar cane, cane workers learned to ferment the run-off or sludge that resulted from the process. Originally called *aguardente de terra* ("strong water of the earth"), this alcoholic byproduct is now the Brazilian national liquor, *cachaça*. Made in the fields and factories of the plantations, *cachaça* became the drink of the workers. In keeping with its humble origins, the liquor's essence was "coarse and insurgent, that rebelled against our palate and the dominant wine" (Camara Cascudo 1983: 47). Despite its impurities and raw taste, *cachaça* was widely consumed.

The folk story about how *cachaça* became the national drink describes how cane was turned into sugar in mills and factories called *engenhos*. Large cauldrons of sugar were boiled and crystallized and later refined. Sometimes the sugar fermented before the process was completed. When this happened, the steam that rose from the cauldrons contained vaporized alcohol that sometimes condensed on the rafters or pipes of the *engenhos*. The story that *cachaça* makers tell is that occasionally slaves were punished by being tied up near these boiling caldrons. Sometimes a poor but lucky slave found himself under a point where the distilled sugar alcohol was condensing and dripping onto his back or arm. He felt the drops and licked them off. He told his fellow slaves about the distilled alcohol, and it became a secret pleasure. The familiar term for *cachaça* in Brazil is *pinga*, which means "drop" from the verb *pingar*, "to drip." The verb *pingar* also refers to the process by which the steam from the still is condensed in a tube and drips down into a container as liquid alcohol. Further stories suggest that the plantation owners/managers learned of the alcoholic byproduct of sugar production and either forbade its production or reserved the product for themselves (De Oliveira Santos 2009).

The Portuguese colonial rulers, unhappy with *cachaça*'s popularity, imposed a law that banned production from 1649 to 1661. The prohibition provoked a popular uprising in 1660, frequently referred to as the *Cachaça Rebellion*. After the rebellion, the prohibitions were lifted, but they were replaced with heavy taxation. Since this rebellion, drinking *cachaça* has taken on additional symbolic values as an expression of patriotism, the worker's pleasure in his product, resistance to the state and the heritage of slavery; it is the archetypal local drink.

Not surprisingly, *cachaça* is a popular but not a sophisticated drink. In fact, *cachaça* has usually had a reputation as a low-class/rot-gut alcohol. Only recently has it risen in stature as distillers have improved the production, removed most of the impurities from the alcohol, and refined the process to produce a smoother and more flavorful beverage. Nowadays, *cachaça* can be sipped like a fine brandy as well as served in cocktail form, namely as the tasty *caipirinha*. In the principal *cachaça*-producing areas, such as the town of Salinas in Minas Gerais, *cachaça* tours and tastings are becoming a tourist attraction. There is also, now, an annual festival celebrating the drink. In Salinas, the local branch of the state university offers a degree in *cachaça* production, attesting to an increase in its desirability as a potential career.

The most famous Brazilian cocktail, the *caipirinha*, is traditionally made with *cachaça*, sugar, and crushed limes. The name for this drink derives from the word *caipira* ("country person" or "hillbilly"). Its name thus evokes its history as a beverage of the rural and poor sector of society. For many years this drink bore these stigmas. In middle- and upper-class venues such as restaurants and clubs, this drink is frequently prepared with vodka instead of *cachaça* (and is called a *caipiroska*, or Russian *caipirinha*), thus separating the drink from its rustic origins and the elite consumers from the hillbillies who invented it. "Oddly enough, for decades, high-end *cachaças* were almost nonexistent in Brazil itself. *Cachaça* was the drink of the people, the 50-cent shot in the corner bar after a long day's work in the cement factory" (Isle 2008). Until recently, *cachaça* was produced for internal consumption only. There were relatively few national brands and many small regional distilleries called *alembiques* (stills). Nowadays there are quite a few national brands and the hundreds of small regional distilleries have become artisanal producers. The making of *cachaça* has gone from backyard and bootleg to artisanal craft. Recent brands have gained a new cachet as a distillate that can match vodka or gin as a premium drink, and in some cases, brandy or cognac as a digestive. New brands are being introduced as the drink is being more widely exported. This growth is evident in Minas, which has become a principal producer of *cachaça* and now rivals the traditional center of the industry in Brazil's Northeast.

Minas is a region that is filled with small, artisanal *cachaça* makers. Tours of these distilleries are advertised along the more rural roads of the state, and visits and tastings have become a profitable tourist attraction. Antonio Rocha, a small-scale *cachaça* distiller from Salinas, Minas Gerais, explained the differences between his family's approach and that of the big distillers.

Our fermentation takes 25 hours. The big producers ferment in 40 minutes. They use catalysts like sulfuric acid or *fuba* [a kind of corn flour] to speed fermentation. "When it comes to the cane itself," he added, "the big producers harvest mechanically, crush the cane, steam it to extract the juice, then crush it again and steam it again, until there's effectively not the remotest dribble of sugary juice left." The Rochas cut their cane by hand to ensure that they get only the best parts and crush it just once in their water-wheel-powered crusher. He says "it's the difference between tossing the whole orange in the blender and drinking that, or squeezing it by hand." The statement struck me as one of the better analogies I've ever heard for industrial-versus-artisanal production. (Isle 2008)

The stores and markets in the *cachaça*-producing area are filled with hundreds of different labels, many of which are not nationally known. Bars and restaurants, however, are beginning to have a larger and more discriminating selection of artisanal labels. Whereas upper-class and refined people once insisted on *caipiroskas* to denote their distinction and elite status, now they can call for a fine *cachaça* such as *Beija Flor* to signify their exalted status.

Distinction

The new gastronomic trends in Brazil have refigured some of the inequities of a previous age. Race, class, and ethnicity are classic sociological categories for distinguishing groups of people. As each of the chapters in this book shows, these criteria play a significant role in how and what people eat, how they choose, and what they get out of the foods they eat. New criteria, however, are emerging that cross-cut these more classic parameters and show new ways in which individuals and groups define themselves. These modes of identification and discrimination follow the criteria that Bourdieu outlines in the construction of distinction (Bourdieu 1984).

Chefs and diners are complicit in constructing a new elite composed of people who self-identify as sophisticated through their evaluation of taste. Appreciation of food, in both its classic and more innovative forms, has emerged as an important criterion of education and sophistication (Trubek 2008). Participating in the new gastronomy, patronizing the acclaimed restaurants, and discerning the innovative tastes and textures of the celebrity chefs has become a stepping stone to the new social elite. These elite sophisticates not only gain distinction by participating in new culinary trends and trying new dishes, they help determine the standards by which judgment and evaluation of others is achieved. Such trendsetters set the bar for achieving status but are also vulnerable to shifting values and changing cultures that may lead the status hierarchy to seek distinction elsewhere. Such insecurities help impel the leading chefs and culture creators to constantly evolve, discover, and create.

–8–

Conclusions

Brazil as a Nation

Riding buses across Brazil, one sees the landscape outside the window often transforming dramatically. The houses and stores, roadside stands, and goods for sale all change form as the landscape and climate alter. One thing, however, shifts very little as one moves from north to south, east to west, region to region, state to state, and that is the roadside bus stops where the passengers all descend to use the facilities and eat a quick meal. Whether big or small, shiny or decrepit, these pit stops all offer the same fare, a buffet of semiwarm foods: rice, beans, greens, a dingy salad, *farinha*, some form of chicken in pieces, and a small barbecue on which sausages and pieces of beef lie grilling. The ever-present *cafezinho* is here as well. This food is a common denominator around the country. Travelers across Brazil can thus usually find food that is familiar and satisfying, if not always fresh and enticing. While eating they can watch (or turn away from) a TV playing familiar programs on the wall or counter. In all these ways, these restaurants evoke the sentiment of *comida caseira*, and some such venues explicitly advertise as such. Wherever the travelers are, no matter how far from home, they can feel assured that the place they are in is still in their comfort zone. It is still Brazil; it is still home. What does this tell us?

It serves to emphasize one of the main points of this book, which is that food is one of the key factors that help define a sense of identity and a feeling of social belonging. In the case of Brazil, despite its many distinct regions and identities, a strong commonality extends across the country, across all levels of regional, national, and family identity. Even when an individual is far from home, he or she shares that common identity with those around him or her, eating in the same roadside restaurant. Brazilians all speak the same language, eat many of the same foods, watch the same TV shows, and most root for the same (or rival) teams. The uniform food at bus stop restaurants acts as a common denominator of national identity and becomes embodied in the travelers through the food they eat.

Some aspects of shared identity and culture take on increased importance as individuals re-identify as national citizens rather than as local actors. Some of these national characteristics have been described earlier in this book. The national myths of Brazilian culture extol the history of the country as a mixture of indigenous, European, and African ancestry, and these identities are embedded in stories that surround *feijoada*, *cachaça*, and *moqueca*, all foods that today contribute to creating aspects of shared identity. The Brazilian perspective on these relations diverges from the dominant discourse in the United States, despite the similar confluence of cultures between the two nations. Brazilians make an explicit equation between the three components, which is not true in the United States. In the United States, the Afro-American cuisine is classified as a regional cuisine whereas in Brazil it is often elevated to a national level. The myth of the poor and enslaved using their skills to raise a plain and homey dish, like *feijoada*, into a gastronomic treat creates a model for the nation. This unity is further enhanced by the belief that *feijoada* is eaten by "everyone" at the same time on the same day, thus allowing everyone to share this national essence and identity. The imagined community takes on embodied form as collectively consumed essence (Anderson 1991). Chapter 5 queries this egalitarian assumption without denying its mythic value.

National identity is not just a sense of political community, although it is frequently associated with a political entity such as a state. Nationality is a sense of identity shared by a population that calls upon a common history, language, dress, and cuisine to emphasize a sense of shared belonging and perspective. As the only country in Latin America to have been a Portuguese colony and thus to have Portuguese as its national language, the Portuguese language is a particularly important defining characteristic that sets Brazil apart from its neighbors.[1] As with many large countries, Brazil is a society of many disparate elements that also maintains an awareness of itself as a nation. The mythic history of the colonial and slave past, the belief in the social policy of racial democracy, and the pride in the current economic boom are all aspects of this identity. Although Brazil has no national costume that people don for Independence Day or other festivals, nevertheless Brazilian clothing does reflect this shared sense of identity through the prevalence of clothing in the national colors. More people wear green and yellow on a daily basis than any in other country I know; this is particularly true in the midwestern and rural parts of the country but noticeable in all regions. This is not a case of a national dress or school uniform, but a show of belonging through embodying one's affiliation to the nation by wearing the colors of the flag and the uniforms of the national soccer team. The same sense of identity is also bound up with national foodways.

The identification of the citizen with the nation as a whole, on a level transcending that of more limited regional, ethnic, class, or gender identities, is critically involved in the formation of nationalism. Nationalism is not simply a matter of national identity, but an active commitment to the potency or preeminence of that identity over other loyalties both internal and external. Material and symbolic media play essential parts of such a transcendent identification of the citizen with his or her nation as a whole. Food and cuisine is one of the principal media in Brazil through which this transformation from local to national identification is achieved.

The links between regions and the encompassing nation are constantly constructed and modified as regions develop a clearer articulation of particular cultural and social factors that give each region its distinctive flavor and identity. Emphasizing interesting and unique aspects of an area's history, culture, and resources is important for many reasons, not the least of which is tourism. Regional identity is important for the strengthening of communities, for artistic endeavors, and mechanisms of economic development. As aspects of Brazilian culture, food, music, television programs, and economic models become better known outside Brazil, global awareness of the country and its potential as a tourist destination increases. More people want to visit the country and explore its regions for themselves.

In this context, regional and national identities are dialectically related and can mutually reinforce their social and economic potential. Regions, however, may put stress on their relation to the nation by pursuing divergent interests or seeking to dramatize their strengths, resources, and different identities in ways that threaten the stability of the national in the international arena. Such developments may also put regions at odds with the central government or dominant elite of a country. In Brazil some of these conflicts emerge around the issues of Amazonian development. Regional groups and actors may turn to support networks beyond the nation to assist them in determining their own future (Keck and Sikkink 1998). International units like the European Union or the Organization of American States may sometimes support subgroups or regions against the policies of the nation state. But regions may also lose some of their integrity and distinctness as people and businesses move and shift across the country and its frontiers. Local residents move out and adapt to the subcultures of their new homes; outsiders may move in, bringing different cultures and traditions from other parts of Brazil or even other countries. Patterns of migration, as we have seen, often change the daily practices of the migrants. What were once taken-for-granted attitudes and orientations become more marked. Festivals, foods, and religious customs become consciously cultivated tokens of an identity more than simply an unconscious, embodied part of who one is.

Foods are both easily transported from and particularly salient aspects of the identity of a particular place and the people who live in it. Portuguese, Angolans, Nigerians, Germans, Japanese, Italians, and many others moved to Brazil and sought to re-create the familiar in the strange. The layouts of towns, the street names, the house styles, and the kitchen gardens all retain some influences of former lives in different places. But not all migrants are free to recreate their former homes in these new contexts nor are all familiar materials available in them. As the generations pass, old and new become recombined in a variety of ways. New foods, different climates, and cultural influences have all affected the ways people eat.

People and Food on the Move

This book has focused on the local habits, foods, and values of parts of the great Brazilian nation. Although focused on the micro level of who eats what and why, much of what people eat is what is available and affordable. In a globalized age, food is often transported around the world and imported food may be cheaper than local food. In fact, much of the cheaper food Americans and Europeans consume may be imported from Brazil. Beef and chicken are longtime exports from Brazil and now soy (*soja*) is being grown for export primarily to China. Brazil's concentration on developing large-scale industrial production has made Brazil a major global food exporter at the same time that hunger and malnutrition continue to pervade much of its population. Discrepancies in wealth and access to land are enormous and increasing, although they have begun to be redressed by the social programs of the Worker's Party government. As we have seen, these inequities have led to large-scale internal movements of people.

Many factors influence the movement of people, some violent, some more benign. In Brazil, poverty and the need to provide for a family have been key stimulants. The cyclical droughts across the northeastern section of the country act as an impetus for individuals and families to migrate from the hinterlands to the towns and cities. Other factors ranging from the consolidation of big land tracts to the opening of land for settlement, from the availability of domestic or industrial jobs to the absence of local employment, have also impelled people to move. As with the migrations of people into Brazil from overseas, the internal migrants also carry cultural and social patterns to their new destinations.

Feeding Migrants

Regional food instantiates the phrase "the taste of place" (Trubek 2008). As a product of a certain climate, geography, soil, production style, and so forth, it may evoke a *terroir*. Those who grow up eating their place through such foods and dishes see them as embodied qualities producing an identity, or at least an affiliation, with those who also feel themselves a product of the same environment. The Paraense saying about *açaí* captures this belief: "Come to Pará and stop, drink *açaí* and stay." Consciously or unconsciously, the Paraenses equate food and identity. These associations are embedded in family meals, Sunday dinners, festive or ceremonial repasts, and the longing or nostalgia one feels for that familiar taste when far away.

As people and ingredients move, one can see the ways that particular foods (*moqueca, pato no tucupí, mocotó, tutu a mineira, sushi,* etc.) embody properties of "culture-richness"; they evoke emotions and connections in those who have long-term associations with them. The absence of such foods often causes longing or nostalgia (*saudade*) as experienced by Da Matta's daughter in the conversation reported in Chapter 1. Sutton terms these emotions *synesthesia* or the union of the senses (2005), a powerful feeling that combines memory, longing, and sensory desire. Not all foods are so tied to a place; some are easily transportable and can absorb the meanings of a myriad of new consumers from a range of social groups: examples of such foods are *farinha, pão de queijo,* and *feijoada.*

This familiarity with the *terroir* of a region evokes a "synesthesia" of emotions, smells, tastes, and desires (Walmsley 2005). To appease this longing, migrants from a region often congregate at eating places where food, music, and dialects all converge to re-create a sense of their home region and the communal belonging they felt there. The *Feira do Norte* in Rio de Janeiro instantiates this essence, but so also do small family restaurants or bars if regionally or ethnically oriented, like the ones Ana Luisa Trajano frequented when she moved to São Paulo. Regional chefs (and cooks who cater to migrant workers) interpret their work as engendering an atmosphere where clients can ingest that sense of place and its accompanying regional feelings of belonging and identity and feel comforted by them. They are not just providing nourishment; they are fostering identity, community, and mental well-being. Even in regions of dense concentrations of ethnic communities, such as often describe Italian, German, or Middle Eastern populations in Brazil, members of these communities gather periodically at restaurants, festivals, or church dinners to reinforce a sense of belonging through the sharing of food, music, language, and even dress styles. The clientele participates in these activities that reinforce traditional identities even after many generations of settlement in Brazil.

The goals of these regionally oriented chefs contrast with those of chefs in metropolitan centers who fuse ingredients from multiple regions and varied international traditions to create their culinary offerings. These chefs scan the country for regional ingredients and recipes to titillate their customers to a different end. This type of chef is not trying to embed his or her clients in a particular atmosphere or identity, however congenial it might be. Instead he or she is trying to select and combine disparate regional products into a new integrated whole. In this sense, these chefs are creating a national cuisine that draws inspiration from components originating from widely dispersed areas around the country, but refigures them into a new whole that is not reliant on the meanings and values each may have in its place of origin. This national cuisine emerges from travels, conversations, and experimentation, but it is identified not with its places of origin but with a transcendent space that encompasses all parts of the country and creates a new national totality.

The food involved in these transformations thus has a multivalent quality. The composition of a food or recipe encompasses the taste, texture, aroma, and contrasts of its ingredients, but also encapsulates the meanings, values, memories, and *terroir* that it conveys from producer to consumer. When these foods are eaten in the locale of their origin or principal source of distribution, they embody all these qualities for those who habitually enjoy them. When foods or dishes are exported from their place of origin, the totality of these components becomes more fragile, and aspects begin to fade or transform. When *açaí* leaves the Amazon, we have seen how it morphs from one type of food eaten in specific contexts, such as a home or food stand for breakfast, lunch, or dinner, to other, equally specific but quite different, contexts such as the beach or gym in the South of Brazil, or in the form of a smoothie or health food drink in Europe or the United States.

Nationalism and Internationalism: From Migration to Emigration

Much of what makes a nation is created through comparison with and distinction from other nations. Therefore, nationalism and internationalism are two sides of the same process much as regionalism and nationalism are. Brazil becomes a known entity, not just a lived experience, through its image abroad. This image is conveyed in part by restaurants serving as ambassadors. People, foods, ideas, and dishes all undergo transformations as they move outward from their regions or even their country of origin. Although Brazilian restaurants are not as ubiquitous as Chinese, Thai, or Mexican ones on the international scene, they are increasing in number as Brazilians continue to emigrate and settle elsewhere in the world. As we have seen with internal migrations within Brazil, restaurants accompany migration for several reasons. The most obvious is to feed those who are far from home and who have *saudade* for the tastes, smells, and sounds of that homeland. Restaurants of this sort may cater to a regional population and provide more universalized Brazilian fare such as the rice, beans, and grilled meat of *a prato feito*, accompanying this principal dish with favorites such as *pão de queijo*, or *kibe*, or the more regionally specific dishes such as *feijão tropeiro*, *mocotó*, *bobó de camarões*, or *sarapatel*. Many restaurants respond to a multiethnic or multiregional community by offering a sampling of dishes from different regions to appease the varied clientele. The selection of one dish to stand for each distinct region may become a template for a "national" restaurant offering a composite menu that, through this selection, constructs a new overarching category: "Brazilian food."

A second reason that restaurants follow migration is the culinary and small business niche open to migrants in a new place. Restaurants are a relatively easy business to initiate and maintain, although they are devilishly exhausting to manage and sustain. These restaurants provide for and, in many cases, exploit the labor of an extended family. As Goody (1998) describes for Chinese restaurants, migrants' restaurants are often cheaper than their competition and open longer hours than more conventional restaurants (as are their neighborhood stores). Furthermore, many international cuisines are heavily based on vegetables and starches and use meat as a garnish or flavoring. Such dishes are less expensive to prepare than traditional Euro-American fare (Goody 1998). The combined result of these factors is to allow new businesses a competitive edge and a foothold in a new place. In so doing, they also expand and deepen the reach of their traditional regional and national cuisines, and, in this case, further the globalization of Brazilian food.

Ironically, however, the Brazilian-style restaurant that has taken off in the United States is the *churrascaria* with its heavy emphasis on assorted grilled meats and its bounteous buffet. This aspect of Brazilian cuisine appeals to the American market, which tends to be weighted toward meat consumption. Another dimension of the *churrascaria* that appeals to Americans is its "all you can eat" offerings.

Churrascarias are opening in the United States with increasing frequency. Some are branches of Brazilian restaurants such as *Porcão* or *Fogo de Chão* and have multiple venues, while others are smaller, independent establishments. The independent restaurants are more likely to be found in niche markets like Cambridge or Somerville, Massachusetts, and New York City's Williamsburg, Brooklyn, where there are large Brazilian communities. For many outside the Brazilian community, the *churrascaria* is their sole experience with Brazilian cuisine.

Compared to many ethnic restaurants, Brazilian ones in the United States tend to be more upscale, focused on meat and copious buffets. They are neither cheap nor do they convey the atmosphere of most Brazilian restaurants in Brazil, which tend to be small and, often, noisy places. These American *churrascarias* are, instead, fine dining experiences in a more formal setting. There are, of course, exceptions, but, at least in the United States, these tend to be confined to areas with large Brazilian populations. In other countries such as England or Portugal, one can find more casual Brazilian eateries offering sandwiches, *pão de queijo*, and rice and bean dishes.

A different kind of restaurant with a Brazilian flair is *Sushi Samba*, with various branches around the United States. This restaurant showcases the multiethnic aspect of Brazil by offering fusion food with a Japanese flair. However, it also serves classic Brazilian dishes like *moqueca* and *churrasco*. This restaurant is more urban, youthful, and international in style than the strictly national atmosphere of the *churrascaria*. With its sleek décor and catchy music, it appeals to a youthful clientele.

Another way that Brazilian food is disseminated around the world is through diplomatic channels. An interesting book highlights meals served at several Brazilian embassies. These formal meals are designed to introduce foreigners to Brazilian cuisine. The food in this book is remarkably less elegant than most menus in fine dining restaurants. Each menu provides a three-course meal: one begins with a soup or appetizer; proceeds to a main dish, such as bull's tail stew or *moqueca*, or rice and beans with reconstituted dried meat, and finishes with a fruit-based dessert such as *mousse de maracujá* (passion fruit mousse). Not super-sophisticated, these banquets succeed in offering an honest taste of Brazil in an authentic and proud way (Autran 2006).

Bringing the International into Brazil: Culinary Tourism

Despite these various ways that Brazilian food is exported and globalized, it remains a relatively unknown cuisine in ethnic and gastronomic circles. Brazilian restaurants do not yet have the cachet that many other international restaurants do. Moreover, arguably even the products that have achieved renown, such as *açaí*, *guaraná*, or barbecued meat have done so by shedding their cultural meanings. In fact, many of these ingredients are valued for their natural, rather than their social, content as described in Chapter 4.

The invisibility that afflicts this rich and varied cuisine is not unique to Brazil. The majority of Latin American cuisines are relatively unknown in the United States and Europe. Only recently have the foods of Colombia, Peru, and Argentina become somewhat familiar to gourmet consumers outside of their respective countries of origin. It will be interesting to see if gastro-tourism begins to flourish in these countries as the fame of their comestibles increases. The speed with which Brazil is cultivating a national cuisine and making it known to the world is increasing, and celebrity chefs like Atala, Troisgros, and Martins, are active agents in the process. This process, however, is still nascent; Brazilian food and cooking tours are few and far between, and at least one such venture disappeared between 2007–2008, indicating that the market for such ventures is neither guaranteed nor necessarily close to comprising sufficient demand to accommodate the rush to invest and establish new businesses in this sector. At the moment Brazil is gearing for huge influxes of visitors for the World Cup Games in 2014 and the Olympics in 2016. The tourist market will be creating multiple programs to entertain and accommodate the flood of spectators and sports aficionados. At that time, much of the world will be introduced to the food and drink of Brazil, in what may be more authentic presentations, both as direct consumers of this cuisine and through the indirect but wide-reaching and effective mechanism of international media coverage. Brazilian food, therefore, may soon become a globally known and desired world cuisine.

Bom Apetite!

Glossary

Abobora	Squash or pumpkin of multiple varieties
Açaí	The fruit of the palm tree *Euterpe oleracea*
Açaí na tigela	A frozen pulp of the *açaí* fruit served with bananas and granola
Acarajé	A dumpling made of mashed beans fried in *dendê* oil served with *vatapá* and dried shrimp and hot sauce
Adoçante	A sugar substitute
Aipim	Nontoxic manioc tubers, formerly called sweet manioc
Alembique	A copper still for making *cachaça* and other distilled beverages
Alimentação	Nourishing and satisfying food
Angu	Maize porridge
A quilo	"By weight"; a type of restaurant in which you pay by the gram of food
Azeite de dendê	Red palm oil from the *Elaeis guineensis* palm
Bacuri	Fruit of the *Platonia disambiguation* tree used for ice cream, custards, and sauces
Bahia	A state of the Northeast region of Brazil
Baiana(o)	A woman (or man) from Bahia
Baião-de-dois	A pea (bean) and rice dish from the Northeast of Brazil
Barraca	A stall or shack for selling food or goods
Batida	A blended cocktail made of a variety of fruit juices and *cacheça*
Bloco	A group of followers or fans of a music group
Bobó de camarões	A Bahian dish made of manioc purée and shrimp cooked with *dendê* oil
Bolo	A cake
Burití	Fruit of the *Mauritia flexuosa* tree eaten as a fruit and used as an oil
Cá	"Here"
Caboclo(s)	Mixed-race Brazilian, often white or black mixed with Indian heritage living in rural regions
Cachaça	A distilled liquor made from sugar cane
Café da manhã (regional)	Breakfast

Cafezinho	Espresso coffee, a little coffee
Caipira	"Hillbilly"
Caipirinha	A cocktail made of *cachaça*, limes, and sugar
Caldo	Broth or puréed soup
Camarote	A balcony or theater box; a balcony overlooking a *Carneval* parade
Candomblé	An Afro-Brazilian religion
Capixaba	A person or thing from the State of Espirito Santo
Capoeira	A martial art developed by slaves that uses dance and music
Carimã	Cake of manioc flour (the flour also called *carimã*)
Carne do sol	Preserved meat exposed to the sun and preserved with salt
Caruru	A Bahian dish made of okra
Cerrado	The high savannah region of the midwest area of Brazil
Chapa(s)	A griddle or grill
Charque	Dried meat, jerky
Chicha	Fermented beer made of manioc
Churrasco	Barbecue
Comida	Food and/or a meal
Comida caseira	"Home cooking"
Coração	"Heart"
Cuia	A gourd
Cupuaçu	Fruit of *Theobroma grandiflorum* tree; delicious and healthy, described as a superfood, it is used in ice creams, custards, juices
Doce de leite	Caramel pudding made of boiled condensed milk
Doces	Sweets or desserts
Efó	Bahian dish made from a plant called the cow's tongue
Empregada	Domestic worker, a cleaner or cook
Espetos	Homemade fireworks, also a sharp, pointed stick
Farinha (de mandioca)	Flour made from grated manioc tubers
Farinha de agua	Slightly fermented manioc flour
Farinha de trigo	Wheat flour
Farofa	Toasted *farinha* often with butter, may be mixed with meat, eggs, or onions
Farta	"Filling" or "satisfying"
Favela	Shantytown on the edge of urban areas
Fazenda	A ranch
Feijão tropeiro	Trooper's beans, dried beans cooked with dried meat and water
Feijoada	A bean and meat stew

Feijoada completa	A bean and meat stew served with rice, greens, oranges, and salsa
Feita na hora	"Made to order"
Frango com molho pardo	Chicken cooked in its own blood, a dish cooked throughout the country
Frango com quiabo	A dish popular in Minas Gerais made with chicken and okra
Fuba	A fine cornmeal
Garota de tacacá	A (young) girl who makes and sells *tacacá* soup out of street carts
Goiabada	A fruit paste made from guava fruit
Goma	Manioc starch
Guaraná	A fruit of the *Paullinia cupana* plant; high in a caffeine-like compound, it is found in a popular soft drink and energy drinks
Guarani	A major subdivision of the Tupi indigenous tribes
Guisado	A stew
Jabuticaba	Fruit of the *Myrciaria cauliflora* tree; a sweet fruit often used to make jams
Jambú	Leaves and stem of the *Acmella oleracea* plant; the leaves and flowers give a sensation like a small volt of electricity
Jeito (dar um jeito)	"A dodge," to get around a rule or problem
Juçara	Another name for the *açaí* palm
Kibe	An Arab dish, called *kibbeh* in the Mideast: a fried croquette stuffed with minced beef or lamb and bulgur or rice
Ki kayapó	earth oven
Lá	"Over there"
Lanche	A snack
Largo	An open space or plaza
Latifundios	A large, landed estate
Maçaxeira	Another name for nontoxic manioc, formerly known as sweet manioc
Mães pretas	Literally "black mothers," used to refer to nurses who raised white children
Malocca	A large communal house in indigenous communities
Mandioca	Manioc tuber
Maniçoba	A stew made of stewed manioc leaves and dried and smoked meats
Maniva	Manioc leaves used in the stew *maniçoba*
Maracujá	the passion fruit, *Passiflora edulis,* eaten as a fruit and drunk as a juice

Masa	Dough made of flour, corn, or manioc
Milho branco	White corn
Mingau	A porridge made of manioc, tapioca, corn, or wheat
Mocotó	A stew made of cow's or calves' feet
Moqueca	A fish stew made in Bahia with coconut milk and *dendê* oil
Mulatinho	Brown or red bean, literally a diminutive mulatto
Nordestino	A person from the Northeast of Brazil
Oca	A communal house in some indigenous communities
Orixá(s)	A pantheon of deities in the Afro-Brazilian religion of *Candomblé*
Oxalá	The *Candomblé* diety of creation and peace sometimes associated with Jesus
Oxum	The *Candomblé* goddess of beauty, love, and wealth
Paçoca	A Northeast Brazilian dish made of dried beef and manioc flour
Pamonha	A tamale-like dish of cornmeal and a filling steamed in a corn husk
Pão de queijo	A baked biscuit made with manioc flour and Minas cheese
Pastel (pl. Pasteis)	A snack made of cheese or meat in a dough that is deep fried
Pato no tucupí	A Paraense dish of duck cooked in *tucupí* sauce
Pelorinho	A pole (pillar) that was used a place for punishment or whipping
Pequena cidade	Literally a small city, used to refer to one's hometown in the hinterland
Pimenta de cheiro	A small, yellow hot pepper from Pará
Pipoca	Popcorn
Piquí	A fruit of the *Caryocar brasiliense* tree filled with small, barbed thorns; used in numerous Goiana dishes
Pirão	A polenta-like purée made with manioc flour and *dendê* oil
Pirarucu	An enormous fish native to the Amazon River, *Arapaima gigas*
Prato feito	The prepared or "ready plate," a common meal made of rice, beans, manioc, pasta, and a small piece of meat
Priprioca	A highly fragrant plant from the Amazon
Puba	Another name for manioc flour
Resgata	Rescue operations, often used for reviving traditional cuisines
Roças	A small garden plot
Sabor Selvagem	A Paraense NGO dedicated to saving traditional food and cuisines
Salgado(s)	Savory snacks
Samba	A Brazilian dance and musical genre
Sarapatel	A Northeastern Brazilian dish made of pork tripe and other organ meats
Saudade	A deep emotional state of nostalgia and longing

Sesta	A nap or siesta
Tacacá	A soup made of a broth of *tucupí* with dried shrimp and *jambú* leaves
Tacacaeiro/a	A *tacacá* vendor
Tapiocarias	A restaurant or stall selling crepes made of tapioca and a filling
Telenovelas	TV drama series that runs six nights a week for six to eight months and has a huge national audience
Tempero	Seasonings
Terreiro	In *Candomblé,* a venue for the worship of deities; it often includes a plot of land and a house of worship
Terroir	The special characteristics that the geography, geology, and climate of a certain place, which when combined with social practices of care and production, confer upon particular types of produce, giving them a distinctive taste; sometimes called "the taste of place"
Tipiti	A woven tube used to squeeze the poisonous juice out of grated manioc; it narrows as it is stretched
Tiquira	A liquor made from fermented manioc grains
Tomar	"To drink"
Trigo	Wheat
Tucupí	A broth made from the poisonous juice of the manioc plant that is fermented, boiled, and seasoned so it is no longer poisonous
Tupi	One of the main ethnic groups of Brazilian indigenous people
Tutu a mineira	A Mineiran dish made of mashed black beans that are recooked with bacon fat
Ver-o-Peso	The large food and goods market in Belém, Pará
Vitamina	A health drink made of juice and vegetables
Xangô	The *Candomblé* deity of war, bravery, and politics
Ximxim de galinha	A Bahian dish of chicken cooked with *dendê* oil and cashews
Yansá (Iansá)	*Candomblé* Goddess of wind and nature
Yemanjá	*Candomblé* Goddess of the sea

Notes

Chapter 1 — Introduction

1. Donna Goldstein, an anthropologist, describes how making and serving and eating lunch with her *empregada* became an untenable situation, and she had to end the employer/employee relation for the friendship to develop.
2. A *telenovela* is a series that runs nightly for six days a week for up to six months on TV and becomes part of the contemporary culture.

Chapter 2 — Is Bahian *Moqueca* Just Fish Stew?
Food and Identity in Salvador, Bahia

1. Several of the classic dishes in the Bahian repertoire are prepared widely in the Northeast and North of the country (*vatapá*, *caruru*, *mingau*, etc.), but they often eliminate the key African ingredients that are most strongly associated with Bahian food. *Dendê* oil is the most renowned of these components.
2. The *Festas Juninas* or June Festivals are a month-long celebration of Saint Anthony, Saint John, and Saint Peter. This prolonged festival includes music (mostly *forró* and *quadrillas*), dancing, plays, and food.
3. There was a fancy catalog of parts of the exhibit available in one of the market stalls, but this stall was extremely hard to find; we just found it by accident. The catalog was very expensive and was probably not widely purchased.
4. Different gods and goddesses of the *Candomblé* religion have different colors, days, and realms over which they watch.
5. Bahian chicken, a bread and *dendê* dressing, fried dumplings, okra, *farofa dendê*, white corn, yams, beans, and popcorn.
6. The Catholic saints most closely associated with Africa and the patron saints of children.
7. *Capixaba* is the term used to denote an inhabitant of the state of Espirito Santo.
8. Despite this implication, Espirito Santo is not a purely white state. Although slavery was never as important in E.S. as it was in Bahia, there are many Afro-Brazilians in the state, migrants from the neighboring states of Minas Gerais and Bahia.
9. *Capoeira* is a traditional martial art performed to music and thought to have a slave origin. Although it has now spread across the country and the world, and into white, urban, middle-class, and upper-class communities, its roots are backcountry and street fighting (Lewis 1992; see http://www.capoeira-school.be/e/orixas.php).

10. In this sense, these clubs of dancers resemble the *ensaios* of *samba* dancers who enter the *Carnaval* competitions in Rio and São Paulo. The Northeastern groups may rehearse as determinately as the *ensaios*, but their staging is nowhere near the elaborate productions of the *samba* groups.

11. A *bloco* is a group who follows a particular band in the procession. They pay to be allowed inside the rope that demarcates the official fans from those on the street who enjoy all the passing bands.

Chapter 3 — Pará's Amazonian Identity: Manioc Six Ways

1. *Guaraná, Paullinia cupana.*

2. *Ver-o-Peso* means "See the weight" and refers to the regulations that were imposed on the market long ago.

3. This is beginning to change, as chefs in other parts of Brazil begin to utilize the ingredients from diverse parts of the country in a new cuisine, perhaps a new national cuisine. See Chapter 7.

4. These components are the cyanogenic glycosides linamarin and lotaustralin that can become hydrocyanic acid.

5. Tubers that have been grown in nontoxic environments are called by a different name. In Brazil these tubers are called *aipim* or *macaxeira.*

6. *Tipiti* is an indigenous term that has been incorporated into Brazilian Portuguese as the term for this type of manioc press.

7. Some of the other components of manioc such as starch and paste are also widespread since they are used in a variety of manufactured products, but are not singularly recognized as manioc.

8. One of these, however, is an indirect reference since it is "to have one's car windshield broken by a falling mango." This is matched by several other mango references such as to "fill a basket with mangos falling from the trees" and to "suck a mango down to the pit."

9. The other qualities include "never eating mangos when you have a fever," "to have the habit of climbing an *açaí* palm," "to complaining about the price of *açaí* but to buy it every day anyway," to "drive forty kilometers to drink coconut water at Icoaraci (a nearby town)," to "stuff oneself with *papunha* with coffee," to "drink a gourdful of *tacacá* during the hottest time at three in the afternoon," and to eat *maniçoba* and *pato no tucupí* on the *Festa de Círio*.

10. "Do it, do it girl, / Let us go do it without stopping, / You are now my *tacacá* girl, / Scrape, scrape manioc, / Squeeze it in the *tipiti*, / Separate the *tapioca*, / Catch the *tucupí*, / Prepare my *tacacá* / As delicious as *açaí*."

11. This big indoor fairground has dozens of restaurants, but the others all served specialties of the Northeast region such as *mocotó* (stew of horse's hoof), *sarapatel* (stew of intestines and kidneys), *baion a dois* (beans, peas, and rice) and not those of the Amazon region.

12. *Beiju* is usually made of *tapioca* but can also be made of the manioc flour itself.
13. Similar to our hot breakfast cereal Cream of Wheat.
14. *Pimenta de cheiro* is a small, round yellow pepper that is quite hot and is omnipresent on Paraense tables, often as a hot pepper oil.

Chapter 4 — *Açaí*: From the Amazon to the World

1. *Extractivist* is the term used for peasants who live in the Amazon and farm small subsistence plots for food. They supplement their living by extracting various resources like rubber, brazil nuts, and *açaí* from the forest in a sustainable way. Some of the new forest reserves have been designated as "extractive reserves," which permit this form of resource utilization.
2. *Açaí* fruit of the palm tree *Euterpe oleracea* is common in floodplain areas of the Amazon River. When ripe, the berries are dark purple and about the size of a blueberry. They contain a thin layer of edible pulp surrounding a large seed.
3. This potion is said to contain quantities of *guaraná*, which serves as a stimulant. *Açaí* is also attributed with powers of potency.
4. "I went and planted, / And so you were planted, / In order to invade our table, / To supply our house, / Your destiny was drawn, / By the hands of the spirit of the forest, / Under the care of the goddess, / Whose touch is very soft, / You are a plant that drives people crazy with passion, / Male-female of the living tree stump, / Where *Oxossi* makes his post, / The slenderest of the palms, / But a woman swollen with blood, / And a man of much blood, / You give yourself to the core (seed), / And your fruit goes rolling, / To our lazy gatherers, / You deliver yourself as a sacrifice, / Holy fruit, martyred fruit, / You have the gift of being much, / Where others have nothing, / Some call you *açaí* tree, / Others call you *juçara*, / Put *tapioca*, / Put *farinha de água*, / Put sugar, / Don't put anything, / Or drink me like a juice, / I am more than a fruit, / I am the taste of Marajó, / I am the taste of Marajó."
5. One English translation of this saying goes: "Take a trip to Pará, I daresay, One drink of assay and you'll stay."
6. The Black brothers who founded the company Sambazon, which imports *açaí* into the United States, first encountered *açaí* on a surfing trip to Brazil and were so taken with the drink they began their importing and distributing business.
7. Recently Oprah Winfrey and Rachel Ray have sued to have their names removed from the multitude of websites that have cited their endorsement of this food and its fabulous properties (Colapino 2011).

Chapter 5 — "Home Cooking" from the Heartland:
The *Comida Caseira* of Minas Gerais

1. *Piqui* is a fruit with a thin layer of flesh over a core of barbed spines. Eating it is a dicey proposition since puncturing the core can lead to an explosion of painful

barbs in one's mouth. This fruit is cooked in or served with rice as festive components of the regional cuisine.

Chapter 6 — *Churrasco a Rodízio* and *Feijoada Completa*:
The Culinary Production of an Imagined National Community

1. *Feijoada* is also made and served on Wednesdays but that does not evoke the same unity and is more of an individual matter.
2. *Carne do sol* is very popular in the Northeast. It is preserved through salting and drying, although not (as the name implies) through drying in the sun. The meat is air dried in a shelter for several days and the dried exterior protects the softer interior. The meat is soaked for several hours before use in dishes, most commonly sautéed with onions and often mixed with sautéed *farinha (farofa)* in a dish called *paçoco*. In contrast to *carne do sol*, *charque* is also dried meat that resembles jerky (the two terms are cognates) and must be soaked in several changes of water and then stewed, not sautéed. *Charque* comes from the Southern Pampas cattle country while *carne do sol* is more prevalent in the Northeast. Both are traditional ways of preserving meat.
3. In the Amazon, the bean is replaced by the long, stewed *maniva* leaves of the manioc plant.
4. A *feijoada* is an event in which *feijoada* is the raison d'etre for the get-together. The dish names the event.
5. *Carioca* is the adjective used to describe people or things from Rio de Janeiro.
6. Caldwell (2007) describes how social movements in Brazil are trying to get Afro-Brazilians to identify as *pardo*, "mixed race," or *preto*, "black," rather than to self-identify as higher on the white spectrum. Because people self-identify, the census figures are quite varied. The figures for black in the 2006 census had the population at 12.9 million or 7.4 percent. The mixed-race population for the same census was 78.8 million or 42.6 percent ("Brazilian Demographics," *Wikipedia*, http://en.wikipedia.org/wiki/Demographics_of_Brazil#Black_Brazilians, accessed September 30, 2011).
7. The maid did get a day off during the following week as compensation, and I believe her husband received some money for his labor.

Chapter 7 — The Chemistry of Identity:
Cooking up a New View of a Nation

1. SENAC is a vocational training school in hospitality and gastronomy, a federal government institution with branches throughout the nation.
2. This is one of the twenty-two species in the rice genus *Oryza*, *Oryza glumaepatula*. It grows from Cuba to Mato Grosso (Scientific Electronic Library Online, Brasil, http://www.scielo.br/scielo.php?script=sci_arttext&pid=S1415–47572007000300017, accessed August 15, 2011).

3. *Jabuticaba* is a fruit tree on which the fruit grows all over the tree, on the trunks and branches. It is named after the land tortoise (*Jabuti* in the Tupi language) because tortoises congregate under the trees when the fruit is ripe and falling off.

4. D.O.M was named the seventh-best restaurant in the world (and the best in South America) in April 2011 (Anon. 2011).

5. *Priprioca* is an Amazonian root that he uses instead of vanilla in many of his desserts. This root combines the smell of patchouli (often used as a sachet to scent clothes) with marijuana but when distilled or submerged in alcohol produces an interesting and evocative flavor (http://www.youtube.com/watch?v=9u50s6v PMCQ, accessed January 28, 2012).

6. In fact, many of the cuisines represented in this buffet could be seen as representative of Brazilian fusion foods descended from the large variety of immigrant populations in the country. Japanese, Italian, Chinese, and German immigrants have contributed to the national "food scape."

7. Many non-cookbooks, such as this one, also now offer recipes to entice the reader.

8. The numerous cookbooks on healthy eating, Italian, Chinese, and Thai cuisine are not bilingual, suggesting they are just for the domestic market.

9. Father Antonio Vieira was a seventeenth-century Portuguese priest who served as a missionary in Brazil. He was an advocate for the indigenous people and later for the African slave population. He was accused of being involved in the *Cachaça* Rebellion and was recalled to Portugal but was later allowed to return to Brazil.

Chapter 8 — Conclusions

1. This distinction was brought home to me by the comments of a woman who had left Brazil during the twenty-year dictatorship between 1964–1986. She described herself as having gone to Latin America. In her mind that was a region distinct from Brazil. This is a common sense of difference among Brazilians.

References

Açaí. (2011a). "Brazilian Acai Berry Destroys Cancer Cells in the Lab." *Andy Branka.com.* Available at: http://www.andybranka.com/sciencebehindfruits.htm. Accessed April 1, 2012.

Açaí. (2011b). *Optimally Organic.* Originally available at: http://www.optimallyorganic.com/?gclid=COu377fM9aECFUjE3Aod9wzGEg; now available at: http://shop.optimallyorganic.com. Accessed May 30, 2011.

Açaí. (2011c). "The Truth about Oprah, Dr. Oz, Acai, Resveratrol, Colon Cleanse and More." *Oprah.com.* Available at: http://www.oprah.com/health/The-Truth-About-Oprah-Dr-Oz-Acai-Resveratrol-and-Colon-Cleanse#ixzz1qoMTApma. Accessed April 1, 2012.

Acevedo Maria Rosa Elizabeth, and Edna Maria Ramos de Castro. (2004). "Black Peoples of the Trombetas River: Peasantry and Ethnicity in the Brazilian Amazon." In *Some Other Amazonians: Perspectives on Modern Amazonia*, ed. Stephen Nugent and Mark Harris, pp. 37–56. London: University of London Press.

Albala, Ken. (2007). *Beans: A History.* Oxford: Berg.

Anderson, Benedict. (1991). *Imagined Communities: Reflections on the Origin and Spread of Nationalism.* London: Verso.

Anonymous. (2006). "Feel the Power of the Amazon." Available at: www.universaltaste.com/fruit.htm. Accessed June 1, 2006.

Anonymous. (2009). "The Origin of the Acai Name." *The Acai Fruit.* Available at: http://the-acai-fruit.com/origin-of-the-acai-name. Accessed March 31, 2012.

Anonymous. (2011). "D.O.M. Restaurant." *Wikipedia.* Available at: http://en.wikipedia.org/wiki/D.O.M._(restaurant). Accessed October 30, 2011.

Anonymous. (2012a). "Festa Junina." Available at: http://en.wikipedia.org/wiki/Festa_Junina. Accessed April 1, 2012.

Anonymous. (2012b). "The Legend of Acai." *Brazil Botanicals.com.* Available at: http://brazilbotanicals.com/the-legend-of-acai.aspx. Accessed March 31, 2012.

Appadurai, Arjun. (1988). "How to Make a National Cuisine: Cookbooks in Contemporary India." *Comparative Studies in Society and History* 30(1): 3–24.

Atala, Alex. (2003). *Por uma Gastronomia Brasileira.* São Paulo: Editora Bei.

Atala, Alex. (2007). Personal communication. São Paulo, July 12.

Atala, Alex. (2012). "D.O.M." Available at: www.domrestaurant.com.br. Accessed October 30, 2011.

Atala, Alex. (n.d.). *The Creative Process of Alex Atala in His Restaurant D.O.M.* Privately published by Givaudan.

Atala, Alex, and Carlos Alberto Dória. (2008). *Com Unhas, Dentes e Cuca.* São Paulo: Editora SENAC.

Autran, Christina. (2006). *Sabores do Brasil: Receitas da Embaixada.* Rio de Janeiro: Editora Record.

Barbosa, Livia. (2012). "Rice and Beans and Beans and Rice: The Perfect Couple." In *Rice and Beans*, ed. Richard Wilk and Livia Barbosa. Oxford: Berg.

Barthes, Roland. (1968). *Elements of Semiology.* New York: Hill and Wang.

Baumann, Gerd, and Andre Gingrich. (eds.). (2004). *Grammars of Identity/Alterity: A Structural Approach.* Oxford: Berghahn Books.

Bosisio, A. (ed.). (2000). *Culinária Amazônica: O sabor a natureza.* Rio de Janeiro: Editora SENAC Nacional.

Bourdieu, Pierre. (1984). *Distinction: A Social Critique of the Judgement of Taste.* Chicago: University of Chicago Press.

Brillat-Savarin, Anthelme. ([1825] 2011). *The Physiology of Taste: Or Meditations on Transcendental Gastronomy.* New York: Vintage.

Brondízio, Eduardo S. (2008). *The Amazonian Caboclo and the Açaí Palm: Forest Farmers in the Global Market.* New York: New York Botanical Garden Press.

Brubaker, Rogers, and Frederick Cooper. (2000). "Beyond 'Identity.'" *Theory and Society* 29: 1–47.

Burns, E. Bradford. (1993). *A History of Brazil.* 3rd ed. New York: Columbia University Press.

Caldeira, Teresa. (1996). "Fortified Enclaves: The New Urban Segregation." *Public Culture* 8: 303–28.

Caldwell, Kia Lilly. (2007). *Negras in Brazil: Re-envisioning Black Women, Citizenship, and the Politics of Identity.* New Brunswick, NJ: Rutgers University Press.

Camara Cascudo, Luiz da. (1983). *Historia da Alimentação no Brasil.* 2 vols. São Paulo: Editora Itatiaia Limitada.

Carioca, Gabriela. (2008). Personal communication. Belém, October 1.

Carneiro da Cunha, Manuela, and Mauro Almeida. (2000). "Indigenous People, Traditional People and Conservation in the Amazon in Brazil: Burden of the Past, Promise of the Future." *Daedalus, Journal of the American Academy of Sciences* 129(2): 315–38.

Carney, Judith A. (2001). *Black Rice: The African Origins of Rice Cultivation in the Americas.* Cambridge, MA: Harvard University Press.

Cockburn, Alexander. (1977). "Gastro-Porn." *New York Review of Books*, December 8, pp. 119–27.

Colapinto, John. (2011). "Strange Fruit: The Rise and Fall of *Açaí*." *The New Yorker*, May 30, pp. 37–43.

Cupuacu. (2009). www.cupuacu.com/. Accessed April 10, 2012.

Dalva e Dito Restaurant. (2011). Available at: http://www.dalvaedito.com.br/restau
rante.htm. Accessed October 30, 2011.

Da Matta, Roberto. (1964). "Comida and Alimentação: A Structural Analysis." Unpublished manuscript.

Da Matta, Roberto. (1986). *Explorações: Ensaios de Sociologia Interpretativa.* Rio
de Janeiro: Rocco.

Da Matta, Roberto. (1987). *A Casa e a Rua.* Rio de Janeiro: Guanabara.

Da Matta, Roberto. (1991). *Carnivals, Rogues, and Heroes.* Notre Dame: University
of Notre Dame Press.

Da Matta, Roberto, and David J. Hess. (eds.). (1995). *The Brazilian Puzzle.* New
York: Columbia University Press.

Davidson, Alan. (1999). *The Oxford Companion to Food.* Oxford: Oxford University
Press.

De Lima, Maria Dorotéa. (2010). "Patrimônio cultura: os discursos oficiais e o que
se diz no Vero-o-Peso." In *Ver O Peso: Estudos antropológicos no mercado de
Belém,* ed. Wilma Marques Leitão, 69–102. Belém: Universidad Federal do Pará.

De Oliveira Santos, Bernice. (2009). Personal communication. July 1.

De Roberts, Pascale, and Lucia van Velthem. (2009). "Consumo e valorisação de alimen-
tos tradicionais amazônicos em um centro urbano (Belém–Pará)." *Anthropology of
Food* S6(December). Available at: http://aof.revues.org/. Accessed January 30, 2012.

Doría, Carlos Alberto. (2012). "Beyond Rice Neutrality: Beans as *Patria, Locus and
Domus* in the Brazilian Culinary World." In *Rice and Beans,* ed. Richard Wilk and
Livia Barbosa. Oxford: Berg.

Dos Santos, Aldaci Dadá. (2005). *Tempero da Dadá.* Salvador, Bahia: Editora Cor-
rupio.

Eakin, Marshall C. (1997). *Brazil: The Once and Future Country.* New York: St.
Martin's Press.

Edmonds, Alexander. (2010). *Pretty Modern: Beauty, Sex, and Plastic Surgery in
Brazil.* Durham: Duke University Press.

EMBRAPA. (2005). *Cassava: The Bread of Brazil (Mandioca: O Pão de Brasil).*
Brasilia: EMBRAPA.

EMBRAPA. (2011). *Arroz e Feijão.* Brasilia: Liveria EMBRAPA.

Ezekial, Paulo. (2006). "Interview." March 17.

Fajans, Jane. (1997). *They Make Themselves: Work and Play among the Baining of
Papua New Guinea.* Chicago: University of Chicago Press.

Fernandes, Caloca. 2000. *Viagem Gastronômia através do Brasil.* São Paulo: Editora
SENAC.

Ferreira, Luciana. (2010). "Garota de Tacacá." Personal communication. April 12.

Foster, Nelson, and Linda S. Cordell. (eds.). (1992). *Chilies to Chocolate: Food the
Americas Gave the World.* Tucson: University of Arizona Press.

French, Jan Hoffman. (2009). *Legalizing Identities: Becoming Black or Indian in
Brazil's Northeast.* Durham: University of North Carolina Press.

Freyre, Gilberto. ([1933] 1986). *The Masters and the Slaves: A Study of Development of Brazilian Civilization*. New York: Alfred E. Knopf.

Fry, Peter. (1977). "Feijoada e Soul Food: Notas Sobre a Manipulacão de simbolos etnicos e nacionais." *Ensaios de Opinao* 2(2): 44–47.

Gillam, Reighan. (2012). "The Revolution Will Be Televised: Afro-Brazilian Media Production in São Paulo, Brazil." Unpublished Ph.D. dissertation. Department of Anthropology, Cornell University.

Goldstein, Donna. (2003). *Laughter out of Place: Race, Class, Violence, and Sexuality in a Rio Shantytown*. Berkeley: University of California Press.

Goody, Jack. (1982). *Cooking, Cuisine and Class: A Study in Comparative Sociology*. Cambridge: Cambridge University Press.

Goody, Jack. (1998). "The Globalisation of Chinese Food." In *Food and Love: A Cultural History of East and West*, pp. 161–71. London: Verso.

Hamilton, Cherie Y. (2001). *Cuisines of the Portuguese Encounters*. New York: Hippocrene Books.

Harris, Jessica. (1992). *Tasting Brazil: Regional Recipes and Reminiscences*. New York: Macmillan.

Harris, Jessica. (2011). *High on the Hog: A Culinary Journey from Africa to America*. New York: Bloomsbury.

Holston, James. (1989). *The Modernist City: An Anthropological Critique of Brasilia*. Chicago: University of Chicago Press.

Hughes, Marvalene. (1991). "Soul, Black Women, and Food." In *A Woman's Conflict*, ed. J. R. Kaplan, pp. 161–76. Englewood Cliffs, NJ: Prentice-Hall.

Hugh-Jones, Christine. (1978). *From the Milk River: Spatial and Temporal Processes in Northwest Amazonia*. Cambridge: Cambridge University Press.

Hugh-Jones, Stephen. (1996). "Bon raison or mauvais conscience." *Terrain* 26(March): 123–48.

Isle, Ray. (2008). "Cachaça: The Spirit of Brazil." Available at: http://www.foodandwine.com/articles/cachaca-the-spirit-of-brazil. Accessed August 15, 2011.

Junqueira, Lígia. (1977). *Receitas Tradicionais da Cozinha Baiana*. Rio de Janeiro: Ediçoes de Ouro.

Keck, Margaret E., and Kathryn Sikkink. (1998). *Activists beyond Borders: Advocacy Networks in International Politics*. Ithaca, NY: Cornell University Press.

Kernbeis, Dulce Marli. (ed.). (2007). "Festas Juninas: 64 Gostosuras Típicas." Special edition of *Receitas Sabores* 3(15).

Kramer, Jane. (2011). "The Food at Our Feet: Why Is Foraging All the Rage?" *The New Yorker*, November 21, pp. 80–91.

Kugel, Seth. (2009). "In São Paulo, Brazilian Cuisine Is Back on the Table." *New York Times*, May12. Accessed April 1, 2012.

Kugel, Seth. (2010). "Açaí, a Global Super Fruit, Is Dinner in the Amazon." *New York Times*, February 23. Available at: http://www.nytimes.com/2010/02/24/dining/24acai.html?scp=1&sq=%E2%80%99A%C3%A7a%C3%AD,%20

a%20Global%20Super%20Fruit,%20Is%20Dinner%20in%20the%20
Amazon%E2%80%99%20%20&st=cse. Accessed April 1, 2012.

Leitão, Wilma Marques. (2010). *Ver o Peso: Estudos antropológicos no mercado de Belém*. Belém: Universidad Federal do Pará.

Lessa, Barbosa, Humberto Meideiros and Adolfo Alberto Lona. (1999). *Do Pampa a Serra: Os Sabores da Terra Gaúcha*. Rio de Janeiro: Edição SENAC National.

Lewis, John Lowell. (1992). *Ring of Liberation: Deceptive Discourse in Brazilian Capoeira*. Chicago: University of Chicago Press.

Lopes, Thelma Pereira. (2009). Personal communication. July 4.

MacClancy, Jeremy. (2004). "Food, Identity, Identification." In *Researching Food Habits*, ed. Helen Macbeth and Jeremy MacClancy, pp. 63–73. Oxford: Berghahn Books:

Maranhão. (2010). "Tiquira." June 16. Available at: http://nossomaranhao.word press.com/2010/01/30/vai-uma-tiquira-ai/. Accessed June 16, 2010.

Martins, P. (2005). *Culinária Paraense: Coleção Sabores do Brasil*. Belém: Instituto de Educação e Cultura da Amazônia.

Martins, P. (2009). Personal communication. October 2.

Marx, Karl. (1978). "The German Ideology: Part I." In *The Marx-Engles Reader*, ed. Robert C. Tucker, pp. 146–200. New York: W. W. Norton.

Masciola, Gabriela. (2007). "Cachaça." Unpublished manuscript.

Mintz, Sidney. (1985). *Sweetness and Power: The Place of Sugar in Modern History*. New York: Viking.

Mintz, Sidney. (1996). *Tasting Food, Tasting Freedom: Excursions into Eating, Culture, and the Past*. Boston: Beacon Press.

Nugent, Stephen, and Mark Harris (eds.). (2004). *Some Other Amazonians: Perspectives on Modern Amazonia*. London: University of London Press.

Oliveira, Ofir. (2011). Personal communication. June 28.

Pace, R. (2009). "Television's Interpellation: Heeding, Missing, Ignoring and Resisting the Call for Pan-National Identity in the Brazilian Amazon." *American Anthropologist* 111(4): 407–19.

Papeta. (1979). *Pratos da Bahia e Outras Especialidades*. Rio de Janeiro: Edições de Ouro.

Pinduca. (2009). "Garota do Tacaca." Available at: http://www.youtube.com/ watch?v=q8nauM_2viE. Accessed April 15, 2010.

Postais de Minas. (n.d.) *Saboreando a Culinária Mineira*. Belo Horizonte: Postais de Minas.

Radel, Guilherme. (2005). *A Cosinha Praiana da Bahia*. Salvador: Editora Idéia Nova.

Radel, Guilherme. (2006). *A Cozinha Africana da Bahia*. Salvador: Editora Idéia Nova.

Reichmann, Rebecca. (ed.). (1999). *Race in Contemporary Brazil: From Indifference to Inequality*. University Park: Pennsylvania State University Press.

Ribeiro, Jose. (1962). *Comida de Santo e Oferendas*. Rio de Janeiro: Folha Carioca Editora S/A.

Roldan, Mary. (2009). Personal communication. November.

Roseberry, William. (1996). "The Rise of Yuppie Coffees and the Reimagination of Class in the United States." In *The Cultural Politics of Food and Eating: A Reader*, ed. James L. Watson and Melissa L. Caldwell, pp. 122–43. Oxford: Blackwell.

Rural, G. (2009). "Tacacá." Available at: http://www.youtube.com/watch?v=9tVunJ86Cm0. Accessed April 15, 2010.

Santos Neves, Luis Guilherme, and Renato Jose Costa Pacheco. (2002). *Dos Comes e Bebes do Espírito Santo: A Culinária Capixaba no Hotel Ilha do Boi*, pp. 104, 107. São Paulo: Editora SENAC.

Scheper-Hughes, Nancy. (1992). *Death without Weeping: The Violence of Everyday Life in Brazil*. Berkeley: University of California Press.

Sigueira, A. D. (2010). "Local Food Preference and Global Markets: Perspectives on *Açaí* Fruit as *Terroir* and a Geographic Indicator Product." Paper presented at the *Food in Blooms: Cross Pollination and Cultivation of Food Systems, Cultures and Methods* Conference, Bloomington, Indiana, June 5–9.

Sjorslev, Inger. (2004). "Alterity as Celebration, Alterity as Threat." In *Grammars of Identity/Alterity: A Structural Approach*, ed. Gerd Baumann and Andre Gingrich, pp. 79–100. Oxford: Berghahn Books.

Skidmore, Thomas E. (1993). *Black into White: Race and Nationality in Brazilian Thought*. Durham: Duke University Press.

Skidmore, Thomas E. (2010). *Brazil: Five Centuries of Change*. 2nd ed. Oxford: Oxford University Press.

Spittler, Gerd. (1999). "In Praise of the Simple Meal: African and European Food Culture Compared." In *Changing Food Habits: Case Studies from Africa, South America and Europe*, ed. Carola Lentz, pp. 27–42. Australia: Harwood Academic.

Sutton, David E. (2005). "Synesthesia, Memory, and the Taste of Home." In *The Taste Culture Reader: Experiencing Food and Drink*, ed. Carolyn Korsmeyer, pp. 304–16. Oxford: Berg.

Tannahill, Reay. (1973). *Food in History*. New York: Stein and Day.

Terrio, Susan J. (1996). "Crafting *Grand Cru* Chocolates in Contemporary France." In *The Cultural Politics of Food and Eating: A Reader*, ed. James L. Watson and Melissa L. Caldwell, pp. 144–62. Oxford: Blackwell.

Trajano, Ana Luisa. (2007). Personal communication. July 13.

Trevisani, B. (2002). *A Cozinha Amazônica*. São Paulo: Editora Melhoramento.

Troisgros, Claude. (2007). *Receitas Originais do Chef*. São Paulo: Larousse do Brasil.

Trubek, Amy B. (2008). *The Taste of Place: A Cultural Journey into Terroir*. Berkeley: University of California Press.

Turner, Terence. (1999). "Indigenous Rights, Environmental Protection and the Struggle over Forest Resources in the Amazon: The Case of the Brazilian

Kayapo." In *Earth, Air, Fire, Water: Humanistic Studies of the Environment*, ed. Jill Ker Conway, Kenneth Keniston, and Leo Marx, pp. 145–69. Amherst: University of Massachusetts Press.

Turner, Terence. (2011). Personal communication, June–September.

Turner, Terence. (2012). Personal communication. January 24.

Van de Port, Mattijs. (2005). "*Candomblé* in Pink, Green and Black: Rescripting the Afro-Brazilian Religious Heritage in the Public Sphere of Salvador, Bahia." *Social Anthropology* 13(1): 3–26.

Vianna Moog, Clodomir. (1964). *Bandeirantes and Pioneers*, trans. L. L. Barrett. New York: G. Braziller.

Walmsely, Emily. (2005). "Race, Place and Taste: Making Identities through Sensory Experience." *Etnofoor* 18(1): 43–46.

Weismantel, Mary J. (1988). *Food, Gender, and Poverty in the Ecuadorian Andes*. Urbana: University of Illinois Press.

Wilk, Richard. (2006). *Home Cooking in the Global Village*. Oxford: Berg.

Zimmern, Andrew. (2009). "Andrew Zimmern Discusses the Cupuacu Fruit on the Today Show." Available at: http://www.youtube.com/watch?v=zjaqB2DLJOs. Accessed March 31, 2012.

Index